AF553832

Homes without Windows

Praise for the Book

'This is a truly remarkable book, a vivid and empathetic portrait of the precariousness of Dalit working-class life that is rich, insightful, very moving and often quite witty too. The narrative is strikingly visual, with superbly rendered descriptions of social behaviour in public spaces: schools, hospitals, offices and, not the least, community toilets. Memorable, too, are the tender portraits of friends and family members, above all of the author's stoic father and his resolute and resilient mother. The translation is sensitive and seamless, making for a compellingly readable memoir, in which elements of hope and humour are always peeping out amidst the struggle and the suffering.' – **Ramachandra Guha**, Indian historian, environmentalist, writer and public intellectual

'Gujarat cannot be known by knowing only Narsi Mehta and Mahatma Gandhi. It cannot even be known by reading about the ghastly communal riots. This is the Gujarat known in literature, history and politics. But the reality of Gujarat cannot be grasped without understanding the deep-rooted caste discrimination. Chandu Maheria's forensic examination of caste segregation takes us to the heart of what Gujarat is, has been. His searing prose makes the intense recollections of a life lived under the shadow of India's age-old curse – the demeaning reality of caste – equal to the most memorable Dalit life-writing. This English translation by the poet Hemang Ashwinkumar brings every word of Maheria's original to life, in all blood, pain, stench and sweat, all like Chandu Maheria's own.' – **Ganesh Devy**, writer, thinker and cultural activist

'A readable and wonderful story of Gujarat seen through the lens of a twofold Dalit activist – a Gandhian in an Ambedkarian complicity. Chandu Maheria invites us into his private space and shares the stories with ascendant prose. It relates to you because it is told in the companionship of truth and purpose. He speaks of life but also of how death feels like a boring act in the calendar of a humourist. Buttered by a highly enjoyable translation, it is a story about the Gujarati chamber of untouchability.' – **Suraj Yengde**, scholar and author of *Caste: A Global Story*

'This elegant collection of essays by Chandu Maheria, translated with verve and grace by Hemang Ashwinkumar, is a study in poetic irony. Recollections of food and shit, festivals and work, worn feet and precious chappals, and the unsung trauma of the monsoon for urban Dalits, sit alongside affectionate and tangential portraits of Gandhi, the author's Ambedkarite father and resourceful mother and various other colourful figures ... Blending humour and sorrow, this is a sharp and poignant reflection on Dalit material life, its meagreness and toil, and equally, on the imaginative and verbal energy that sustains it.' – **V. Geetha**, author of *Bhimrao Ramji Ambedkar and the Question of Socialism in India*

'Chandubhai's writing has long been celebrated in Gujarat for its piercing clarity – penetrating yet free of bitterness, incisive yet humane, unflinchingly realistic yet untouched by social stereotypes. This translation opens the door for English readers to encounter the brilliance of his craft and the authentic world of lived experience he so vividly brings to life.' – **Urvish Kothari**, journalist and writer

Homes without Windows

Chandu Maheria

Edited and translated from the Gujarati by

Hemang Ashwinkumar

JUGGERNAUT BOOKS

C-I-128, First Floor, Sangam Vihar, Near Holi Chowk,
New Delhi 110080, India

First published by Juggernaut Books 2026

10 9 8 7 6 5 4 3 2 1

P-ISBN: 9789353459383
E-ISBN: 9789353454210

Typeset in Adobe Caslon Pro

Printed at Thomson Press India Private Limited

Dedicated to all those
who are selflessly fighting
the battles for rights

Contents

Introduction by Hemang Ashwinkumar *xi*

1. The Mayor's Bungalow 1
2. The Frigging Fuss over a Rotlo 22
3. That Fellow, Gandhido 40
4. Creed, Conversion and Childhood 64
5. Soak Me Through, Damn You! 84
6. A Diwali No Less, That 99
7. Your Chappals, Our Skulls 121

8. Rama Bhagat, an Intractable Atheist 134

9. Sonny of a Sane Mother 151

10. Those Years in Dhoraji 173

11. Sick Homes: A Journey from Life's Dawn to Dusk 197

Translator's Acknowledgements 217

Notes 220

Introduction

'Not a poet, oh no.
A rebel, that's what I wanna be.'

– Chandu Maheria, 'Value of a Poem', *Asmita* (1984)

Dalit literature in Gujarati had a belated beginning compared to its flamboyant start in Marathi and other Indian languages in the 1960s. As a matter of fact, Dalit prose writing began to be practised seriously only after two shattering anti-reservation riots that rocked the state in 1981 and 1985. Once the terms of Dalit writing were set in 1987 through a manifesto included in the first collection of Gujarati Dalit short stories,[1] writers like Dalpat Chauhan, Harish Mangalam and others did substantial work in the genre of fiction, such that Dalit fiction in Gujarati has come of age in the three-and-a-half decades since its inception.

However, the same is not true for Dalit non-fiction, especially for genres like autobiography, memoir, reflective essays, and so on. And of the few works in this category by writers like Dahyabhai Deenbandhu, B. Kesharshivam, P.K. Valera and Vitthal 'Rai', only Kesharshivam's autobiography, *The Whole Truth and Nothing but Truth* (2008), is available in English.[2] Chandu Maheria's memoir comes as a milestone in this incipient tradition and promises to renew and revitalize it through its cultural and political force.

Written and published over the past three decades as standalone essays in literary journals and magazines like *Nireekshak*, *Sarthak Jalso* and *Dalit Adhikar*, and in anthologies of Dalit writing, Maheria's powerful work has remained largely unnoticed in Gujarat by literati and academia alike. Part of the reason for this apathy might lie in Maheria's overarching reputation in Gujarat as a prominent Dalit intellectual, formidable scholar, firebrand activist, prolific journalist and columnist, something that overshadowed his literary persona as a poet, writer and editor. Part of it also has to do with his indifference to the publication of his literary writing until it was cajoled out of him by his close friends and people he trusts (as was the case with the poet Arun Kolatkar).

Born in 1959 in a sprawling family of nine, Maheria spent the first four decades of his life in the chawls of Rajpur, a working-class suburb in east Ahmedabad. This memoir provides a fascinating account of his early academic pursuits and initiation into intellectual and political radicalism amidst dire poverty and crippling privations. That journey crystallized his ideas about power structures in caste society and drove him to search for truth in the interstices of conflicting ideologies. As a teenager, Maheria realized that the emancipation of his community depended as much on the enlightenment of minds as on the struggle for rights. The numerous letters he wrote to newspaper editors, the study circle called 'Valay', which he organized in the veranda of his house in 1976–77, and the teach-ins he hosted for Dalit children in the wake of anti-reservation riots of 1981 under the aegis of the Bhimrao Students' Association – the root of it all can be traced to his zeal for social reform and Dalit empowerment. It was this zeal, he told me, that inspired his decision to remain unmarried and commit his entire life to the battles of ideas and rights.

In the late 1970s, Maheria began to write poems that appeared in *Kalo Suraj*, a journal devoted to Dalit literature founded and edited by veterans like Dalpat Chauhan and Neerav Patel, and in *Naya Marg*, a reputed fortnightly committed to an exploitation-free society. The razor-sharp language and finely whetted sensibility informing Maheria's creative and intellectual production drew the attention of Indukumar Jani, the seasoned socialist editor of *Naya Marg*, and before long, Maheria was actively working with the magazine. In about two decades of this association, *Naya Marg* became a prominent mouthpiece of progressive, liberal politics in Gujarat, and Maheria evolved as a formidable Dalit voice. During this period, he edited two seminal collections of Dalit poetry, titled *Asmita* [Self-Identity] (1983) and *Visfot* [Explosion] (1984); edited collections of critical and creative prose like *Anamatni Andhi* [The Cyclone of Reservation] (1985) and *Madi Mane Sambhare Re* [How I Miss Mother] (1994); and wrote books of reportage like *Sambaradathi Swamannagar* [Dalit Exodus from Sambarada to Swamannagar] (1995) and *Pranprashna Panino* [Water: A Life and Death Question] (1994).

In 2001, Maheria founded Adhikar, an organization that provided enriching intellectual space for discussing Dr Ambedkar's writings and issues surrounding Dalit literature and the Dalit question. Attended by respectable writers and Dalit intellectuals, these weekly soirées aimed to bridge the gap between thought and emotion, intellect and affect, Dalit literature and Ambedkarite ideas and thus, in thirteen years of its existence, broke new grounds in Dalit–Ambedkarite discourse in the state. In 2005, Maheria founded *Dalit*

Adhikar, a fortnightly that remained in print till 2019 and emerged as a major mouthpiece for Dalit rights.

Maheria may be the speaking voice in *Homes without Windows*, but the reader encounters a breathtaking polyphony in the memoir – it features his extended family, his friends across religion and caste, his neighbours, his community and gives us glimpses of a hegemonic Hindu order that has acquired new strength over the years. The memoir unearths, for the first time, the vibrant community life of the Dalits who had migrated after Independence to Ahmedabad from far-flung villages because, as Maheria's father reminisces, 'There was no place for us there, just none. No work, no home, no dignity, nothing. So, consider this place your village. Wherever you get shelter, and a piece of bread is your homeland.'

The harried, unhomed humanity finds a home in the seedy chawls, mushrooming in the shadow of chimneys towering over the industrial city. A home without windows, with a leaky roof, crumbling walls and reigning dark. Even so, the labour settlements, overflowing with people from diverse caste, class, religious and ethnic backgrounds, become a theatre of love and compassion, of communal coexistence amidst caste/class struggles, of unyielding hope in the face of precarity. Maheria depicts a life that, though forged in the crucible of privation, is full of joie de vivre, like the Diwali his family celebrates, a low-key affair, but 'a Diwali no less, that'.

Maheria memorializes the invincibility of human spirit in the figures of his father (Ba) and mother (Ma). The saga of his father's radical aversion to anything superstitious and the extent to which he stood by the truth, as well as his mother's battle against dire poverty and commitment to give her children education and a better life – these are stories of Dalit predicament, but also of resilience and indomitable inner strength. Maheria's long essay on his mother, 'Sonny of a Sane Mother', is a paean of love, devotion and admiration:

> A woman as generous as she was truthful and optimistic, Ma never tired of running around for the welfare of her family, neighbours, remote acquaintances, even random passers-by and thus won glad, grateful hearts, almost in hundreds. Thus,

> my Dahima, literally a sane mother, was Ma to many. 'Is there anything we humans can stake a claim on when we pop off?' was her pet rhetorical question and refrain when someone asked her to just slow down and look after herself.

Personal is political. *Homes without Windows* is suffused with a politics that is neither abstract nor a slave to any ideology. It arises from the lived experience of deprivation and caste-based dehumanization. Maheria's engagement with the canker of caste is gut-churning, literally and figuratively. Scatology becomes a pungent, poignant device in 'The Mayor's Bungalow' to construct a profound and multilayered exploration of the fraught relationship of Dalits with the material, structural reality of toilets and, more significantly, with the idea of shit. The essay unpacks what Slavoj Žižek calls a 'hermeneutics of toilets' in Indian society. The whole memoir, in fact, constructs a powerful critique and a ruthless indictment of this degrading, inhuman social system, but the exceptional clarity of Maheria's vision enables him to seek out the grey in the black-and-white discourse around caste. He espouses a recourse to identity politics but in a way that liberates and humanizes both the oppressor and the oppressed.

His sharp and profound understanding of the politics of naming, shaming and taming led Maheria, in 2008, to take a considered, moral stand in the controversy surrounding Umashankar Joshi's play *Dhed*[2] *na Dhed Bhangi* (1935). The simmering ire and angst of Dalits against the use of proscribed pejoratives like 'dhedh' and 'bhangi' in Joshi's play, which was prescribed for study in an undergraduate degree programme offered by North Gujarat University, had exploded into a major agitation. The play constructed a brilliant, all-out assault on the evil of caste system; not only did it mock the hypocrisy and caste prejudice of Brahmins but also reflexively questioned the internal caste hierarchy among the Dalits. Quite expectedly, the copies of the disputed play were burnt. At the height of the controversy, Maheria approached Joshi and pointed out not just how the slurs in the play subjected Dalit students to anguish and humiliation in classroom spaces but also how they put the well-meaning orientation of the play 'out of focus'. Confronting Joshi, Maheria said,

> The title implies that the Bhangis are dheds among dheds, just as the latter are dheds among the Savarnas. Such logic, in a way, justifies the Savarna disgust and prejudice against the Dalits; it's as if the dheds deserve an insulting treatment because they themselves treat the Bhangis insultingly ... The title of your play looks, at first sight, prejudicial and disdainful though it's quite likely that you might have used it innocently and in good faith.[3]

Maheria's polemic of caste is profound and perspicacious; it respects cross-caste solidarity but is also sensitive to the blind spots of uncalibrated, collective fight. If it does not spare the internalization of the logic of caste by Dalits themselves, it simultaneously exhibits a keen awareness of the prevalence of the worst forms of patriarchy within Dalit society. 'Your Chappals, Our Skulls' describes an incident that took place in Golana village in 1975. In an act of expiation, the Dalit leaders had to walk through the village holding in mouth the chappals, turban and torch of a Kshatriya man who had tried to assert his traditional right over the body of a Dalit woman and was chased away by Dalit youths. The same Dalit men, Maheria writes, expected their womenfolk not to walk past them while wearing a pair of chappals, as a mark of deference to patriarchal norms of propriety and gendered subordination.

The idea of Dalit *biradari* [fraternity/solidarity] that transcends the boundaries of narrowly contrived ethnic or social identities is central to Maheria's polemic. The concept of biradari is a call to solidarity across ideological enclosures, a heartfelt hail to join forces for imagining a common future on a shared, salubrious planet. Such progressive, accommodative politics drives Maheria to realistically assess the role of 'That fellow, Gandhido'[4] in shaping the past, present and future of the Dalit community. This essay is a precious gem in the entire gamut of Dalit discourse on the Mahatma and his philosophy, next in value only to Kannada intellectual D.R. Nagaraj's analysis of the old man's legacy. In so far as the call for forging solidarities is a call to recognizing our common humanity, Maheria's politics of (re)writing the self can safely be called

Gandhian, or that of a satyagrahi, one who holds onto the truth.

The colour of truth is grey, its song always polyphonic, like the Natal Garba that symbolizes the rich histories of communal coexistence and religious intermingling that Maheria traces in 'Creed, Conversion and Childhood'. Maheria brings out the sheer complexity and fluidity of the idea of religious conversion in India. The attitude of the local Dalits, converted to Christianity, to the missionary imposition remains one of suspicion and ambivalence despite the promise of material aid and the liberation from caste hierarchy. Conversely, the Hindu Dalits of Rajpur, Maheria notes, 'Always used the term *deval*, the Gujarati equivalent of a church, to refer to local Hindu temples and shrines. Thus, the assorted deities in the Hindu pantheon like Baliya Dev and Mother Maha Kali sat guiltlessly in their separate churches that we, the Hindu Dalits, visited for worship.' The essay points back to a not-so-distant time when practices of intertwined religious worship and intercultural communion defined the existential realities of a multireligious, multicultural society.

Maheria rues the emergence of a political context in Gujarat that has carved out hard-edged community identities and singularities of being. He brilliantly shows how the project of communal estrangement begins with the partitioning of language use and then leads to segregations and exclusions of hideous kinds. Thus, he shows how the Dalit and Muslim residents of Baharpura in Dhoraji remain *outside* not just of the town but *outside* the imagination of developers and policymakers. In fact, the memoir becomes a site for deconstructing hegemonic discourses of caste, patriarchy, communalism, authoritarianism and neoliberalism that, under the excuse of forging a national 'self', impose immense suffering and dehumanization on the toiling masses. Sadly, a large part of Indian society is made to believe, through institutionalized hate and the politics of fear, that such eviction and exclusion are preconditions for development, for the onward march of history and for re-engineering a home, a homeland and a Hindu Rashtra.

At a time when a crazed nationalist pursuit of such a home has spawned a fear psychosis and an era of precarity, Maheria speaks of his lost world with a sense of nostalgia; his mind keeps returning to it, just as he himself does to his ancestral home in Rajpur, for sustenance and emotional support. The home in Rajpur, aptly named 'Nirant' [a place without terror/ fear], remains Maheria's permanent home; the one in Gandhinagar, where he currently stays, is just 'A Home on Probation', the title of his short essay where he depicts what makes 'Nirant' a home:

> Life in Rajpur's melting pot, overflowing with its attendant ironies and contradictions, retains a lot of its old-world charm; it is still possible here to get a packet of oil on credit, scrounge two free matchsticks, buy tikka-kebab on the street, watch suspense thrillers in Usha-Sheetal Talkies, to enjoy kawwali and mujaras, and buy fat-rich milk from Sharmaji. Here one gets Hemingway and Neruda in the libraries of Gomtipur and Rakhiyal, vibrant discussions in 'Valay', the *karmashila*s [activists] of the Dalit Panthers and CPI(ML) and Dalit poets like Nirav Patel and Dalpat Chauhan.[5]

Translation is linked to the close, intimate act of reading and translating *Homes without Windows* line by poignant line made me feel like a bird, weaving its nest one twig at a time. Maheria's words helped me build a home of hope in a literary context where the great majority of wordsmiths find their tongues paralysed over issues that Chandubhai so boldly and beautifully discusses.

At a time when bulldozers are tirelessly at work in the New India, razing down homes of the poor across castes and religions, this memoir might drive the reader to rethink the kind of home 'We, the people' want to build ourselves. The choice is stark: bulldozer or biradari, destruction or diversity, madness or what Dr Ambedkar called *maitri*. Hopefully, the reader will take a cue from 'Nirant' – Maheria's windowless abode of peace, prosperity and plurality – open the windows of their minds and let it flood over with the sunshine of solidarity and the luminescence of shared dreams.

– Hemang Ashwinkumar

1

The Mayor's Bungalow

Since the day I moved to my new house in Gandhinagar, the capital city of Gujarat, I have been dreaming, curiously enough, of just two things: the police and toilets. The ever-expanding strip of land east of Ahmedabad called Rajpur, a dizzying clutter of working-class settlements, was my original home, native village or homeland, whatever you call it. Decades back, my ancestors had migrated from a village in Kheda district to Ahmedabad. As a child, whenever I asked my father – or Ba,[1] as we called him – how he came to this textile city, he would snap, 'Dragging myself on the arse!', as a familiar bitterness lined his face. At a time when Dalits were not allowed to travel by train, coming to Ahmedabad, trudging down 80 kilometres, household freight and family in tow, and crossing four rivers – Khari, Meshvo, Vatrak and Shedhi – en route, would have been a real ordeal. Tired and troubled over a journey, lasting days on end, they would have just slumped and set up camp in the new city wherever they first encountered something like a human settlement. That's the reason why today one sees a concentration of Dalits from Kheda in suburbs like Maninagar, Khokhara and Rajpur, from Dholaka in Vejalpur, from Dehgam in Naroda and those from north Gujarat in areas like Sabaramati, Ranip and Chandkheda. Sometimes, however, Ba stoically laid out his story, one of the thousands his generation of migrant Dalits had to tell. 'We left the village because there was no place for us there, just none. No work, no home, no dignity, nothing. So, consider this place your village. Wherever you get shelter, and a piece of bread is your homeland.' A textile mill that manufactured fabric for vests and frocks in the neighbouring suburb Rakhiyal was Ba's workplace. Fair to say that back then, a seedy chawl had mushroomed in the lengthening shadow of every single mill chimney that towered over and dotted the tightly packed suburbs in east Ahmedabad. Shameful excrescences on the face of a modern city, those chawls. One such dense, dingy chawl at the intersection of Rajpur and Gomtipur, was called Abu Kasai's chawl, and therein squatted my dumpy little home, built from the scratch and scrap by my grandpa. All these chawls were privately owned and identified interestingly by the names or the surnames of their owners: butcher's chawl, mason's chawl, Modi's chawl, washerman's chawl, Jethi's chawl, Rami's chawl, Dost Muhammad's chawl, Nathuram Dagdu's chawl, magistrate's chawl, judge's chawl, and so on. Again, they housed not just Dalits but also the Savarnas and Muslims prior to the anti-reservation and communal riots of 1981–85 and 1992, respectively. We shared the backyard of our house, for instance, with a Muslim family – Barkat Bibi, her husband who worked as a security guard and their young son. Post Babri, they distress-sold their house at a throwaway price and left Rajpur, never to return. Jains too – you heard it right – stayed and ran provision stores in these chawls.

I think my life shares as deep a bond with my excretory system as it does with my respiratory system, for whenever I jog my memory and drag it to the far end of my early childhood, the odd things that invariably surface on that mnemonic landscape are the sordid toilets of the neighbouring chawl, named after its owner Hiralal. And rightly so. For, as if the question of filling the bottomless pits of hunger was not vexed enough, the daily dilemma of emptying our bowels had made our lives, both personal and social, embarrassing and miserable.

The rub was that our chawl didn't have even a single public toilet attached to it, something that compelled us to use those hellish toilets of Hiralal's chawl. Kids like us could squat anywhere on the footpath outside, but what would the elders do? And what about the women? Our chawl was inhabited in large part by the Rohits, people of the tanner caste, who had migrated from Charotar, a large swathe of fertile land covering districts like Kheda and Anand in central Gujarat. However, the rest of the chawls, including that of Hiralal, were populated by the Vankars, people of the weaver caste, from Mehsana, a district in north Gujarat. Deprived of the social respectability that separate toilets attached to one's chawl brought, we had to sheepishly go relieve ourselves at the Hiralal's. Toilets of their own had got the Hiralalwallas inebriated with a sense of entitlement, so they threw their weight around, name-called us with slurs like the *chanotara*[2] and let go of no opportunity to harass us. We too got even with them by calling them – not publicly, however – bloody *patanwadia*, the people from Patan district.

And all this cheek was for toilets that were no better than hellholes. Can you beat that? Unlike the ones we commonly use these days, the floor of those toilets was not set in marble or glossy, ceramic tiles. With coats of plaster dropping off its walls, the goddamn structures sported big patches of brick-and-mortar design at several places. And in most cases, the lousy excuse for a door had neither a stopper nor a chain latch to boast of. Something that left the squatter on the edge throughout the business ... to the mercy of Lord Rama, if you will. A soiled, soggy chamber pot, flanked by two parallelly placed uneven stones, was all one had in the name of a toilet seat. No marks for guessing, one of the stones would either be broken or on the verge of it, which made the whole human squat installation lean on one side.

Even in such an awkward position, the user literally had to hold fast to the makeshift chain, or whatever that secured the rickety door, lest someone from outside pulled it open, out of innocence or sheer malice. As the wavy line of prospective users grew outside, a howl of protest from the disgruntled and impatient queuers soared, warning the user inside to make haste. At such moments, if someone snitched about such and such chanotaro occupying such and such toilet, the precariously hinged door would be yanked open with a bang and the water in the brass pot, carried for washing and flushing, would be drained with a resounding kick. Despite waiting in the queue till your legs ached, at the time of your turn, if a patanwadia kid materialized – God knows from where – you had to forgo your right to use the loo and give the queue-jumper the right of way. Again, a rowdy Vankar harrying a chanotari, filling her pitcher with water from the public tap, by thrusting his filthy toilet pot midstream and letting it overflow was a common sight. A strange thing to say but it was in these queues that I had learnt my first lessons in social inequality. All these people were extremely beleaguered, a harried lot that had come here to escape poverty, untouchability, oppression and exploitation, and yet they saw hierarchy and hatred as natural ways of being, such that even the slightest breach in the set order resulted in exchanges of expletives and blows. Though not untouchability in its conventional sense, these practices were rooted in direct discrimination, in an ordained difference between the high and the low, that had seeped right up to the bottom of the caste order. One scene in particular comes back to me repeatedly, no matter how hard I try to forget it. The first house at the mouth of our chawl was that of Bala Dhedh,[3] a Vankar from Kheda and thus, a chanotaro for the patanwadia. In the 'thatch' – a kutcha hut – attached to the house stayed Neno Ma'raj, a man of priestly Garoda caste, considered the highest among the Dalits. A mill worker of no consequence, Ma'raj would, in a blatant exhibition of his caste pride, lay his string cot out on the footpath every evening and lounge there like a maharaja, a veritable badshah holding his royal court. At such time, the area became off-limits for everyone, even for a mangy-looking cur. For if the poor thing came up, barking or sniffing, from within the chawl, an affronted Ma'raj would fly into a lion rage, hurl a stick at it and roar, 'Buzz off in, you ... stay in ....' In his exhaustive, eye-opening study of the forms of untouchability, practised by non-Dalits and Dalits (among themselves) in Gujarat, my friend Martin Macwan has pegged the numbers at ninety-eight and ninety-nine, respectively. Where would this kind of untouchability, and its distinctive, discriminatory form, figure in those lists? And in the dragnet of such divisions and sub-divisions, what happens to Dalit biradari, the idea of fraternity and caste solidarity?

I have often wondered why we Dalits use the same word *gandh* [odour] to refer to both fragrance and stench. Perhaps, in the Dalit lexicon, there are no separate terms to define and differentiate between pleasant and unpleasant smells. Thus, for us, everything 'reeked', be it a rose or a vial of *attar*. Even otherwise, how could the dictionary of a people, whose olfactory organs had known nothing but the noisome stench of toilets day in day out, have a luxuriant terminology around fragrance? The public toilets in Rajpur, as elsewhere, brimmed over with excreta almost as a rule. Worse still, the ingenious lot in our locality saw them as a gateway to the nether world for the huge, grey rats they trapped at home. They would come up with their rat traps and release the furry thing into the toilet from the gaps or holes in the rickety door, without bothering with it being occupied or vacant, in the fervent hope that the animal would scurry its way into the cesspit below;

naturally, the sudden entry of Uncle Rat with scary, needle-like whiskers would make the squatters get the hell out of there, their bowels blocked by astonished sphincters. On those dreadful days when the chamber pot surged with excreta, the droppings splashed droplets of shit all over the squatter's body. And when these toilets overflowed – which was almost every other day – the unbearable, rotten stench that permeated the surroundings would send a 'normal' human being into fits of retching. And yet, I don't remember having seen anyone in my community gagging, clipping their nose or pressing a handkerchief against it. Conversely, on seeing the Christian converts cover their noses with their scented hankies as they passed by our locality, Dalit women would giggle among themselves and then quip, 'Oh dear me, look at these hoity-toity Christians, they can't stand this odour!'

Right in front of Hiralal's toilets was a large space where kids from the chawls squatted out in the open. Even today, I shudder as I visualize myself in the daily early-morning ordeal of weaving my way to the toilets through that open space, littered with steaming piles of fresh and stale turds, waiting to be stamped over. Generally, the clutch of Hiralal toilets kept bustling with customers throughout the day, but young girls and women couldn't hope to find purchase any time before the sundown when they stepped out, their water-pots discreetly covered by the loose, flowing ends of their sarees. Most of them squatted with the door left half-ajar and duly guarded by their sisters-in-law or friends who chatted away leisurely as the relief operation went underway. At that tender age, I was at a loss to figure out why the young men of our chawl gravitated towards the toilets every evening as soon as it turned dark. Much later did I realize that going to a restaurant or a public garden for a tryst with their beloveds or just to ogle at them in the hope of striking a romantic liaison was an idea alien to their amorous imagination. All one had to do, they thought, was to stand somewhere near the toilets and stare, from that vantage point, at one's love interest to heart's content. To those young men, the toilets of Hiralal's chawl were nothing short of Love Garden.[4]

The bus stop for Hiralal's chawl was right next to these

squalid toilets. As the buses plied by the Ahmedabad Municipal Transport Service halted and stood purring by them, the college-going boys and girls from the chawls, waiting in the toilet queue, a brass pot in hand, would freeze with embarrassment. What a sorry figure they'd cut before their Savarna classmates who might be on that bus, they thought! For reasons too bizarre for me to unpack, the Savarna youngsters from Rakhiyal and Gomtipur mockingly called our toilet-hugging bus stop 'Hollywood'. Scared of being ragged back at college, Dalit boys and girls from Hollywood got off either at Kamdar or Gomtipur bus stops, which came before and after the Hiralal's, respectively, and walked their way home, up or down.

And I can't even begin to describe the sorry scene the overflowing septic tanks of those toilets created. The faecal matter and reeking water would flood the main road, transforming the whole area into a real hell. Often, the sanitary worker tasked with cleaning these leaking loos would be a skinny female, a widowed or deserted Dalit woman, and the contractor's headman would rudely set her to task of scrubbing, breathing down her neck even if she was ill. I have seen several such women succumb at a tender age to the constant, infective exposure to the dirt and the bacteria those squalid toilets liberally emitted. The fellow would push the poor thing into a rickety-doored toilet, unbothered to check if it was occupied or vacant; thus, at times, the door, carelessly yanked open, revealed a squatting man to the lavatory woman's great embarrassment. The sad-eyed lady would then proceed to clean the whole vomit-inducing thing without a wince, let alone a word of protest. And, by her misfortune, if a local bully or an influential man showed up at that time, he would, by force of habit or in exercise of his manly right, pick flaws in her work, give her a public dressing-down and force her to do the cleaning all over again.

On the eve of Diwali, groups of kids from each chawl would take out a ritual procession holding auspicious *mermeraya*, the tiny holy torches made from sugarcane stalks and auspicious lamps, and solemnly visit houses in their respective chawls one after another. The next morning, on the Gujarati New Year's Day, every household would ceremonially discard *kharkhokhro*, the old earthen water pots and suchlike, and replace them with mint-fresh ones. No quarrel with festive customs, but unfortunately, it was also customary among the chawlwallahs to dump this clutter and debris near the toilets. Some cleanliness buffs, the smart-arsed idiots, went a step further and dropped it directly into the chamber pots or septic tanks, and ensured that the auspicious morning of the New Year was welcomed by surging hearts of choked tanks and toilets. Located at the mouth of the chawl, my house had the luxury of having the footpath for its extended veranda and thus, the most putrid stench from the spillage assaulted us before everyone else. And as luck would have it, my friends Indubhai Jani and Harshad Desai would come over around that time to wish us Happy New Year. The prospect of their visit, otherwise a source of huge delight, would turn us all into a bundle of nerves, thanks to the sweeping reign of squalor. From the break of dawn that day, Ma, the poor thing, would get down to removing the litter of faecal matter with a rectangular tin plate and a broom and wash the area repeatedly with abundant water. But whatever one did, the intractable, head-blasting stink would persist in the air. Ultimately, as always, we would welcome our guests with a nasty niff of shit, to the insolent might of which the bunch of incense sticks fuming inside our home would be no match.

You might find this incredible but using such filthy toilets had a cost attached. Many of you might have learnt about *lagaan*, the system of land revenue, after watching the Oscar-nominated eponymous film produced by Bollywood actor Aamir Khan, but I had the foretaste of the toilet 'cess' quite early in my life. Every month, the assorted goons of Hiralal's chawl turned up at our door to collect what they called 'toilet tax'. Drunk to the gills, those local toughies would let loose a stream of abuses as they demanded the 'relief rent', and if someone made a feeble excuse about their salary being due or delayed, they would fly into a blind rage. The womenfolk of that unfortunate house would then coax and cajole them and finally fall to their feet and beg for mercy, the loose end of their sarees outstretched like a begging bag.

By the time I reached the age of recognition, so acutely aware was I of our toilet trouble that I had made up my mind to resolve it anyhow, first and foremost. Significantly enough, the bunch of efforts I made for the erection of separate toilets for my chawl in a way facilitated my launch into public life.

Eventually, with a sharp increase in the density of population and increased traffic in the area, the state decided to widen Rajpur's main and internal roads. As fate would have it, Hiralal's toilets came within the ruthless sweep of the engineer's plumb line and measure tapes; as a result, two rows of men's toilets were demolished. That day, I and quite a few residents of my locality felt a deep pang of sorrow in our hearts as if it was not the toilets but our own homes that we had lost.

In terms of their general state, even the public urinals around our chawls fared no better than the toilets. Thus, an upper-caste doctor who served in our area went as far as Gomtipur just to take a piss; the reason being, it was difficult for almost everyone, queasy or seasoned, to pick their way through all the dirt and gooey ooze that cordoned the public urinal. In case you made it somehow, the yellowish gunk on the walls inside would exude such terrible, head-blasting effluvium, just don't ask. Similarly, to spare himself the ordeal, another doctor running a private practice in our area had improvised the small wash area in his clinic into a personal urinal; he would draw the curtain of the injection room, squat near the drain and pee but could never in his life muster the courage to use the public urinal, oh no.

Much later, the municipality came up with a scheme to build a dedicated toilet for every single house in the chawls. The collaboration clause of the scheme mandated the municipal corporation and the householder to bear the construction cost to the tune of eighty and twenty per cent, respectively. I vividly remember a funny episode that had taken place while our toilet erection was underway. The hawker woman, who regularly came to our chawl to sell vegetables, had innocently asked my mother, 'Why just one toilet? What about the womenfolk? Won't they need one as well?' Clearly, she had thought that, just like public lavatories, an in-house latrine would have separate arrangement for men and women. When we saw our 'personal toilet' for the first time, complete with a snow-white commode and glossy, tiled floor with a skirting to match, we were literally flabbergasted. Our house had a tin-sheet roof, but the toilet had a ceiling of reinforced cement concrete; the house floor had a thin coat of cement plaster, but the toilet floor was beset with shiny, brand-new ceramic tiles. To be honest, so spick and span was the toilet space that I often felt the urge to take my meals sitting in the toilet rather than in the kitchen.

Thanks to the government scheme, every single house in the chawls got its own toilet, but the remaining toilets of Hiralal's, with their signature slime and grime, remained intact, the standing symbol of a bygone age. Several activists and motivated young men tried their best to get the authorities to erect a community hall, a kindergarten or a chain of shops in their place, but to no avail. Getting the stink out of the way of a Dalit ghetto was just impossible, even unadvisable, it seemed.

Finally in 1997, when a countrywide protest erupted against the defacing of Dr Ambedkar's statue in Mumbai's Ramabai colony, the Dalits of Ahmedabad too called for a *bandh*, a general strike or a lockdown of sorts. As dusk fell, angry crowds of Dalit youth spilled from narrow lanes and streets onto public roads. They were raring to take out their deep outrage one way or the other but were clueless about how to do it. Just then, someone suggested that the demolition of the Hiralal's toilets would be a fitting response to the insult, and everyone, keen on monkey business, went gung ho. Within no time, the toilets were razed, and every single bit of brick, no matter how soiled with flowing shit and piss, was spirited away.

After the demolition dust settled, lengthy deliberations about what to do with the cleared space went underway. Evidently, the chawl had a clear title to the toilet land, and thus, it was the sole and undisputed right of its residents to decide what happened with it. However, while one group had plans of erecting new latrines there, to the other, the whole proposition was pointless as each household in the chawl had its own pucca toilet now. But ultimately 'better' sense prevailed, and it was resolved to construct a pay-and-use public lavatory there. And within a year, the facility came up – big, better and smartly turned-out. Today, the mint-fresh public utility, with whitewashed walls, tiled floor and an entrance flanked by lush potted plants, stands tall at the mouth of Hiralal's chawl. Such is the glitz and glam of the place that one would prefer to use it, not as a place for *shauch* – squat – but as a space for *soch* – thought. But the access to the luxurious lavatory comes at a cost, a rupee for a go, quite something in a context when many textile mills in the city have shut up shop and the residual, small-scale factories too are in throes of recession. Dire poverty and unemployment hold the entire suburb in a vice-like grip with the result that the pay-and-use toilets are hardly ever used. Even today, every time I visit Rajpur, the sight of this new, gleaming utility pricks my conscience. At a time when few houses in the locality could compete with the utility in terms of shape, size and sophistication, what better name could the poor chawl residents have thought up for this bedecked behemoth than the highly creative and shrewd epithet, 'The Mayor's Bungalow'? Yes, we call it the Mayor's Bungalow, and such bungalows have popped up at multiple locations in the city now. Be that as it may, those decrepit toilets of Hiralal's chawl still invade my dreams, jolt me out of slumber and goad me to write something about them under a dim, dazed, midnight lamp.

2

The Frigging Fuss over a Rotlo

Back in 1984, Mahesh Parmar, our family friend, landed a coveted job in a public sector bank. Getting his first posting at a town branch in Mehsana, he began to commute daily by train. In the first few days, he realized that the manager of his bank, Shah Sir, also commuted on the same train. What luck! Pleasant company would take the sting off the tedium of the rush-hour between Ahmedabad and Mehsana, he thought. And before long, Mahesh got absorbed and ensconced in the mesmerizingly unique world of up-and-downers. One day on their way back to Ahmedabad, the manager held out his unlidded snack-box before Mahesh, silently insisting that he try some. As soon as Mahesh broke a sliver of the crispy, crunchy thing in the box, he exclaimed. 'Sir, how does your wife make such paper-thin roti?' Everyone around burst out laughing, more at the man's naivete than his question. 'Parmar, this is not a roti; it's called *khakhra*,' the manager clarified, a shade of smugness lining his face.

That evening, when he came to our house on his routine post-dinner visit, Mahesh looked unusually excited. Without wasting a moment, he launched into a graphic description of his snazzy discovery, a fancy delicacy called khakhra, leaving us all spellbound and fantasizing. Over years, Mahesh has scaled the professional ladder and become a bank manager, affluent enough to dine at a whim in a posh restaurant. But the fact remains that in the mid-nineties, the brittle, flaky eatable, upheld so vigorously as the pride of Gujarat by Narendra Modi, was completely unknown to us Dalits living in the squalid, tumble-down, cheek-by-jowl dwellings in the backstreets of the city, dubbed as the heart of the state. Even today, there would be at least four to five households in my chawl that wouldn't have encountered the thing called khakhra in all their lives, and a dozen or so that wouldn't have tasted it.

Those days of my childhood were the days of utter deprivation, torrid times when every single grain of food meant the world to us. Ba, a textile mill worker, was the sole earner in our large, working-class family of nine – five brothers and two sisters – and raising it on his meagre wage understandably was difficult as hell. A real nightmare.

The crisis of food security loomed so large that even the coarse grain *rotla* made from reddish wheat, provided under 'PL-480 US food aid' programme, had become a luxury for the poor. Food rations were strictly controlled, and one could procure a smidgen of grains, if one were lucky, from those patronizing Fair Price shops, but not before making multiple rounds of the subsidized public ration facility for the poor and pleading with the proprietor. We had to fill the deepening pits of our tummies with thick rotla made from the flour of lowly grains, like millet, sorghum and small-grain or fat rice. At daybreak, Ma patted and baked round cakes of rotla over a desi sigri, fuelled by sawdust, and served one each to us brothers. We hungrily ate our share of the piping hot rotlo with curry and hid what remained of it – generally a quarter – within the folds of our respective quilts, piled on a wooden hope chest, like a prized booty. A stinking quilt, a soiled chest and a quarter of a rotlo, tucked away in that mouldy safe – that's all we knew and had in the name of a bank. A unique rotla bank. Today, a sense of nausea creeps over me as I think of the frigging piece of reeking rotlo and the fact that I ate it with such relish. Be that as it may, would I ever be able to flush it from my memory – that the whole of my childhood was spent clinging to the lure of that food cache?

Most of the men and a handful of women of our chawl worked in the surrounding textile mills that functioned in three shifts. The routine of the chawl life, throbbing day and night with the deep hum of those mills, was organized like clockwork to the mills' schedule of sirens. Ba's shift started at seven in the morning and ended at half past three in the afternoon. The lunchtime was clocked for half an hour, eleven to eleven-thirty. His tiffin would be readied by nine-thirty and delivered by one of us boys at ten sharp when the towering mill gates were thrown open briefly. My day school kicked off in the afternoon, so it mostly fell to me to do the honourable thing of walking all the way from Rajpur to Rakhiyal, the tiffin box dangling in hand. Ba would be at work inside when I reached, so I had to place the tiffin box in the shed, designated for Dalits to dine, and trace my way home on weary steps. But on lucky days, Ba would personally come to receive his lunch at the gate and buy me hot, oily puris, worth five paisa, from the mill's canteen. This was reason enough for me to undertake the long march every day and linger in his shed in the fond hope that he'd come out. All the workers, Dalits and non-Dalits, drudged in those mills together under the same precarity and pressure, and yet their dining sheds were segregated. It wasn't until my teens that I realized why the hyped Marxist unity of workers was missing among those in Ba's mill. Dr Ambedkar was spot on in his analysis of the caste system as a division of labourers rather than of labour, wasn't he?

Yet another memory associated with the mill and the rotlo refuses to budge from the centre of my hippocampus. Thanks to my sedentary government job, I had gotten into the habit of having a cuppa at about four every day at a tea stall outside my office. But often the spectre of distressing childhood memories spiralled up, without any reason or provocation, and messed up my teatime, completely spoiling the taste of the tea I have come to develop an addiction for over years. The story goes like this. Every day at three-thirty, Ba's shift ended. By the time he walked home, it would be a quarter past four. All of us brothers would take our position at the post office on Rajpur crossroads, ready to burst into a sprint at the first sight of Ba in the distance at the bend of the Topi Mill. This was not out of the delight of seeing him after a half-day long absence and to embrace or cling to him the way kids do, oh no. The rat race was to snatch the tiffin from his hand before anyone else did. For the tiffin carried a slice of rotlo, Ba deliberately spared and brought back for us, his ever-hungry boys.

The government's midday meal scheme was yet to be introduced then. But we did get a glass of milk at school every day before classes. My school, a lacklustre municipal primary school, was just a stone's throw away from our home, and those austere times were blissfully innocent of fancy school bags, lunch boxes, multicoloured waterbags or insulated flip-lid sippers. During the recess, I'd shuffle my way back home and have a cup of wishy-washy tea with the hoarded, mouldy slice of rotlo. Things weren't so dismal for everybody in my school, however. A few cliquish kids, who came from faraway chawls, did bring lunch boxes from home and polished them off, sitting in a circle in the playground, classroom or lounging royally on the windowsill, their legs stretched out and eyes soaking the city hubbub outside. Being an ace in academics, I wasn't generally asked by my teachers to run errands like bringing spicy hot pakoras from the modest, hole-in-the-wall shop on the pavement outside. But when I saw my sticky-fingered classmates sampling pakoras on the sly from the order on the way to its delivery and their over-the-top description of the snack's heavenly taste, I burnt with jealousy, streams of saliva flooding my mouth.

Today, I have to follow a diet regimen to keep this old, frail body going, this den of diseases. Fried food is strictly out of bounds for me, but in those years of blooming adolescence, my taste buds craved fried titbits crazily. Oil was a luxury item in our kitchen, something to be bought in minuscule quantities, in a dedicated small bowl or a *toyali*, a handy water pot, from Naran Sheth's provision store, tucked deep inside Jethibai's chawl. And the game was to go shopping for it in the dead of the afternoon when the stingy Sheth settled for his siesta, putting his large-hearted servant in charge of the shop. Puris we got to eat only around the festival of Shitala Satam, that too after lining up in an endless queue before the Fair Price shop under the beating sun and the gathering dark from the afternoon of Nag Pancham to the evening of Randhan Chhath.[1] And to what end, you may ask? Well, for a seer of maida and half a seer of soybean oil or palmolein, whatever was available for a condescending dole-out, to fry hot puris and anoint our craving palates with the oil fizzing over it. The celebration of Randhan Chhath, thus, came at a cost – material, physical and psychological – but it was a small price to pay for the culinary bang and blast.

Even amid absolute privation, Ma and Ba indulged my elder brother, and quite invidiously at that. A privileged eldest son of the family and a veritable lamp of the lineage he ostensibly was. His claim to the lion's share of parental pampering was also due in part to the fact that he studied at St. Xavier's College in Ahmedabad. Ma served him a fried rotlo every morning to break his fast with, but the choosy sir deigned to have just the middle part and leave the oil-rich edges. In a way, it was to our advantage, for Ma then equally divided the edges amongst the rest of us, a leftover breakfast for her leftover sons.

And the kind of breakfast people in those chawls had! Ah! It's beyond anyone's imagination. Only a select few homes could afford the luxury of broken, discarded rusks – those sold in open handcarts – in their breakfast. The rest helped themselves with the leftover from the previous night's meal, mostly a lump of stone-cold khichdi mashed into a cup of scalding hot tea. I remember, once someone in the chawl had innocently admitted to soaking non-veg *pulao* in a tumbler of tea. The poor thing was ruthlessly ribbed for days by the young and the old in the chawl. Catcalls of 'pulao-tea' went up whenever the gentleman passed by. In a similar vein, an entire household in our chawl had come to be called *banti-bavata*, the eaters of lowly grains like broomcorn millet and ragi. The nickname, in all probability, had stuck from the platitude the elderly woman of the house often mouthed: 'One should eat whatever one gets, banti or bavato, without a shout or a pout.' I wonder how the buffets of dire poverty had not blunted a people's sense of humour and even with very little, they could find something to laugh about.

The financial crunch in my family had robbed me of the pleasures of school excursions. The only picnic I went on was in Class 3 to Kankaria Lake and Gandhi

Ashram in Ahmedabad, and that too sadly ended up as a bitter, harrying memory. Every single moment of the picnic flashes before my eyes in raw, graphic detail and immediacy. All students were required to bring their own snacks from home. My elder sister had lovingly packed me my favourite combo, sautéed mashed potatoes and puris, in a *dolachu*, a small, lidded brass bucket. Who was interested in seeing the sites at Kankaria? Not me. My heart was locked inside the dolachu. We reached Gandhi Ashram after noon. Our teachers sat us down in a big circle, asked us to pray and then have the home-brought snacks. Rushing through the prayer, I had hardly unlidded the dolachu when a crow overhead aimed jets of its droppings right on the puris and flew away cawing triumphantly. At the sight of the shit-soiled puris, I burst into tears as the boys around me roared with laughter. Later, a few felt bad about it and gave me something to munch from their snack-boxes. Even today, after all these years, when I step into the cool, lush green of Gandhi Ashram, I begin to smart under a strange, stinging feeling. And then I end up casting about the Gandhi Ashram, not for Gandhi but for that cunning crow.

Sometimes I wonder if the meat-eating of the working-class Dalits, living in those huddled-up chawls, had anything to do with taste or liking. Wasn't it a form of helplessness? An inner compulsion? For a sprawling and plain broke family like ours, the water-soaking mutton was more pocket-friendly and nourishing than the freshest of veggies. As for a dish of spiced lentils and boiled rice, we believed it was meant only for the affluent. Thus, I can count on my fingertips the rare, festive occasions on which I had dal-rice on my plate. Yes, on days we went so broke as to be unable to afford anything for curry, vegetable or meat, Ma asked us to get some dal from the Umiya Shankar Lodge in Gomtipur to go with the rotla, a satisfying meal only she could cobble up. The other-worldly fragrance of that dal, spiked with kokum and peanuts, melted our hearts, but I still remember how the lurking fear of being caught by our non-Dalit classmates in the act of buying dal from the bazar drove us to skulk on the roadside and cut the corners. The mere thought of that sense of shame, laced with a blood-curdling fright, overwhelms me; it sends a chill down my spine even as I write this.

The lodge reminds me of Kalamama's son, Babu. One of his hands, with a slight handicap, looked exactly like a snuffed-out stub of cigarette, so we mockingly called him Bablo butt. Mama was an early widower, so Ma had reared his sons like her own. Babu worked in a lodge in a labouring suburb called Saraspur. Once, by some strange oversight, he stepped into a pan of boiling oil and badly burnt his foot. Ma had nursed him round the clock for days on end. Thus, Bablo had come to develop a soft spot for our entire family, Ma in particular. His job at the lodge was to lug a load of tiffin-boxes on his rickety bicycle and deliver them to existing customers. On days when Bablo butt landed up at our place on his way back from delivery rides, he instantaneously morphed into a respectable Babubhai for us kids. For then he would let us polish off the leftover food in those tiffin boxes. The helpings of tainted, tasted dal, rice, rotis, puris and fried delicacies would make our day, literally. A festive day of Diwali.

In a context where a frigging piece of rotlo became a veritable battleground and a point of hysteric breast-beating, there is no question of me having heard of, let alone tasted, chocolates, you'd think. You're right, but not quite. For I have keen memories of bartering exotic chocolates for money and buying a seer of flour from it. Adjacent to our house in the chawl was a 'thatch', i.e., a kutcha hut, which we had rented out to a man called Tulsibhai who worked as a caretaker of tourist buses of the Ahmedabad Municipal Transport Service. Handing out costly chocolates as welcome munchies to the tourists who hopped on those sightseeing buses was his delightful job description. Of course, some of the chocolates made it to the chawl to be dispensed to us fawning kids in return for errands we so gratefully ran for Tulsibhai. So rare and alien were those pricey chocolates that even the local confectioners of Rajpur were struck dumb when we flashed one to them. Our chawls were filled with mixed castes and classes, harbouring people who struggled to make ends meet and people like my chum Poonam whose family led a life of reckless extravagance and conspicuous consumption. We called him 'an elephant's calf' as a joke on his tubby figure. The elephant was cash-rich, a fact confirmed by the staggering amount of pocket money the calf always had on him. I would sweet talk

Poonam into buying those chocolates in colourful wrappers, but not before clinching the best bargain in which he was made to feel that paying a bomb for those world-class goods was worth it. The money made would then be spent on grocery, toiletries and other essentials for the house.

Today, whenever I see rag-picking kids in cities, I involuntarily begin to seek out my kid-image in their faces. For, in the months of vacation or on days of leisure, I too set out with my friends, a tote bag hanging from my shoulder, on picking expeditions. Not rags but bones. Meat was consumed liberally by the Dalit population in Rajpur, and the bones, once the beefy dogs had their turn on them, lay around in abundance drying in the sun. We picked them through the day under a scorching sun and sold away the bagful to a tin-shed shop outside Santram Colony for whatever was on offer. Without ever picking a bone about the price, that is.

If bones had been a source of income, they had also been a source of public embarrassment to us. One such episode involving a bag of bones had taken place during the prolonged anti-reservation riots of 1981. A long-lasting curfew in Rajpur had crippled our movement, and unauthorized absenteeism in a government job for someone like me had its consequences. As a stop-gap arrangement, we moved to our small row-house in Maninagar, essentially a mixed neighbourhood but dominated by a bunch of 'pure' vegetarians. Days wore on without the situation getting back to normal. It had been a while since we had mutton, and our stomachs had begun to rumble for it. One day, taking courage in both hands, we smuggled some in and relished a spicy, hot mutton-curry to our heart's content. But what to do with the contraband bones? Late at night, we tiptoed out in the street with the load of bones, hidden in a thick polyethylene bag, hoping to dispose it of in a scrub far away from the housing society. As luck would have it, at the society's gate, we ran into a young man out on a walk with his pet dog. Before we could think of an excuse or an escape hatch, the dog pounced on the polyethylene bag and shredded it to pieces. Our guilt tumbled out, drowning us in the sea of shame.

Our life in Rajpur was bleak but not hopeless. Food shortages we suffered were thankfully punctuated by episodes of satiating meals when we stuffed ourselves. During the winter, the same working-class suburb witnessed vendors hawking fish and green garlic. The aroma of mango pickles in the month of May and that of nutrition-rich *vasanu*[2] in December hung over the chawls, almost like a pall, so dense that it cancelled out the odour of overflowing toilets. During the mango season, it was customary among the chawl residents to invite guests, especially their married daughters and her in-laws, and treat them to the whipped pulp of ripe mangoes and rotla. The tradition continues uninterrupted even today among the Vankars in and outside those chawls.

Eventually, the men in my family landed government jobs, thanks to the reservation policy of the state, and the days of deprivation were over. Reminiscing on one's poverty, and worse still, writing about it, has become a matter of embarrassment. It's still something to be discreet about in social conversation. Today, the chawls of Rajpur are part of my past. My extended family live in ease and luxury in fancy colonies in Ahmedabad and Gandhinagar. Ma, in her eighties, now prefers crispy khakhra, what she calls 'Bania roti', as a snack over everything else. When I see my nephews gorging on chocolate bars and ice-cream balls, worth a couple of hundred bucks, without batting an eyelid, a surge of mixed feelings washes over me and sends me scurrying down memory lane in search of my lanky, malnourished body. I have always seen myself in the images of the skeletal kids of Kalahandi. I was literally a bag of bones in my childhood and adolescence, a scarecrow planted in a farm, one could say. Funny as it might sound today, but I often tried to fix a deep-frying pan in my concave stomach in a bid to make it flush with my chest. Today the concave has become substantially convex. Friends and family often cry havoc over it, but I don't care a fig. Because ...

3

That Fellow, Gandhido

I like to wear khadi. It suits my short body and slim build. But Ma doesn't like it a bit, the fact that I wear it. The fabric is anathema to her. Thus, every time I don a khadi kurta and a pair of khadi pyjamas, she takes a dig, not sure at me or my attire, saying, 'You look like a ditto Gandhiyo[1] in this pair.' Ma and Ba had not seen Gandhi anytime in their lives, though he was their contemporary. The world of Ma, an unlettered woman, began and ended with her household and its immediate concerns. In the long years of her marriage, the mantra of her relatively isolated and homebound life was: Be good, do good and feel good. But Ba had heard and learnt a lot about the Gandhi–Ambedkar debate, and even read a bit about their strained relationship. The simmering discontent with Gandhi among the first generation of Dalits who grew up in that era found its way, from time to time, in everything, from a casual talk to a fiery argument that Ma and Ba had in front of us kids. Ma's pet peeve was, 'None but that fellow, Gandhiyo is responsible for erecting these caste enclosures.' Clearly, at the root of her quibble against my partiality for khadi lay the misgivings and mix-ups concerning Gandhi that Ba and the zeitgeist of the era had sown in her mind.

Growing up in the working-class chawls of Rajpur, much of my early education happened in the suburb's Municipal School No. 3-4. Our principal was a man called Balawantbhai Parmar. Though a Dalit by birth, he was a thorough Gandhian. Clad in khadi kurta and khadi dhoti, with a topping of Gandhi cap, when he moved around, the earth shook. Such a disciplinarian the man was. My formative years were spent among Gandhian, Ambedkarite and communist activists and their respective liberal-radical activism. Rajpur of those days, in a way, was a school for learning different political ideologies, a veritable *pathshala* for the pupils of politics.

My exquisitely preserved memories of those vibrant years – the years before the anti-reservation riots of 1981 – are shot through with vivid reminiscences of Gandhi and Gandhism. Thanks to the prolific welfare activities and women-centric programmes the Majoor Mahajan Sangh[2] and Jyoti Sangh[3] organized, respectively, our lonesome chawls received substantial footfall of Gandhian leaders and activists on an almost daily basis. As a result, the atmosphere in the chawls in general remained electric. I received my pre-primary education in a wonderful, Jyoti Sangh-supported Anganwadi, a childcare centre unlike its present-day, state-funded counterparts that are mired in corruption and inefficiency. The service-oriented women of the Jyoti Sangh made repeated rounds of the chawls during summer vacations, unbothered about the baking sun overhead or the squalor reigning all around, to persuade Dalit mothers to send their kids to the Anganwadi. Little wonder that the image of Jasubehn, our loving Anganwadi teacher, in her signature white khadi saree and a winsome smile around her eyes, has survived intact in my mind after all these years when the faces of other teachers have either quietly faded or completely vanished. It was she who first held my hand and helped me trace the lines of Gujarati alphabets and numerals. It was from her that I first learnt the *sarvadharma prarthana*, the all-religion prayer, so close to Gandhi's heart.

Apart from making an effective intervention in the education of poor kids, those women ran intensive campaigns for addiction recovery and women empowerment. Those 'sisters', from posh families and in swank white sarees, plodding the narrow, labyrinthine chawls and selflessly working for the welfare of women and children, had won people's hearts; the chawlwallahs acknowledged and appreciated their single-minded devotion to service to no end. Such close emotional intimacy and deep concern they brought to bear upon their one-to-one interactions with the chawl women that the latter opened their hearts and shared their most personal and familial predicaments with them. Though some of it was recounted in my presence, I was too young then to make a head or tail of it. But today, I realize what really bugged those poor, unlettered Dalit women. Among their grave and grievous concerns, at least two were the most common and somewhat interrelated: the liquor addiction of their husbands and *havahuriya*, i.e., unwanted pregnancy every fifteen months.

The family welfare centres run by the Jyoti Sangh specialized in peaceful and amicable resolution of family disputes, especially those among couples. Family planning and addiction recovery too fell within their zone of operation. There was a squat, simple house in our chawl, unfurnished if one didn't count the table and the chair, and yet well-organized and orderly, the kind I always dreamt of having. The man of that house, the pillar of the family, was an incorrigible alcohol addict, so much so that he was known by the bitchy alias of *lathbo*, a home-made, often poisonous liquor, not just in the chawl but in the entire area. A small-time mill worker as such, he always moved around in starched, khadi clothes, spoke sophisticated Gujarati and possessed deep knowledge of assorted government schemes and the law of the land. When he set out in the morning in glowing, snow-white apparel, he looked a gentleman from top to toe, but come evening, the gentleman would stagger his way back to the chawl, worse for wear. Shantabehn Patel, a senior sister of the Sangh, had made him her sworn brother, just to rid him of the habit of drinking. Tying a rakhi on his wrist in the presence of the chawl residents, she had made him promise, placing the life and love of a sister at stake, never to touch liquor again. Today, when I see small children sell liquor and lurch around in drunken stupor in Rajpur or read about young political leaders like Jignesh Mevani conducting Janta Raids on liquor dens in Gujarat, a mix of painful realization and profound remorse weigh me down, that now no upper-caste woman worth her salt will come forward to swear the addicts as her brothers or sons and wean them off the bane of booze. When I hear well-meaning, social activists (yes, not workers) speak of grinding penury as being the root cause of the evil of alcoholism among Dalits, the staunch Gandhian figures and values, which had bloomed within me in those days and then drowned in the relentless tide of time, shake me up violently. Clearly affronted, they throw down a scary gauntlet to me in the year of Gandhi's 150th birth anniversary.

The school I studied in up to Class 7 had a three-storey building and a sprawling playground. Some of my teachers were Dalits from Rajpur and its surroundings. Our school hosted the Sports Fest of east Ahmedabad region and celebrated national festivals with considerable fanfare. Despite being a consistent topper in my class, I was never given an opportunity to speak publicly at these events unless, of course, it was the school's prayer assembly. Expectedly, the grooming of my speaking and writing skills should have been the singular lookout of the school that had formally enrolled me and the teachers who officially taught me; however, my inborn talent in these respects was first spotted and then lovingly nurtured by those Gandhi pathshalas that afforded me informal, but life-transforming, education.

Back then, the Majoor Mahajan Sangh celebrated Gandhi's birth anniversary and other programmes only in working-class suburbs and with great fanfare. If the old guard of Dalit community leaders are to be believed, everyone in the Mahajan, be it a member, a master or a headman, had pledged themselves to khadi clothes for life. It was a man called Kantilal, a mill worker and home guard who, almost religiously, took me along to these events. The world celebrated Labour Day on 1 May but the Mahajan's May Day dawned on 4 December, the Sangh's foundation day. So what if every single hamlet in the whole wide world observed Gandhi's birth anniversary on 2 October? The Mahajan's Gandhi Jayanti fell on Rentiya Baras, the man's birthday as per the Vikram Samvat calendar. Such was the institution's commitment to Gandhi's word.[4] As a part of these celebrations, huge public meetings were held where various competitions for mill workers' children were organized. True to my temperament and expertise, I'd participate in elocution and essay-writing competitions and always win household essentials like hankies, towels and bedsheets in prizes. The precious lessons in public speaking and discursive writing I received in and through this Gandhian institution later took me so far that I represented my school in an interschool elocution competition, held at Matruchhaya High School, Gomtipur, and received a copy of *The Story of My Experiments with Truth* as a prize from Babubhai Patel, the then chief minister of Gujarat.

Majoor Mahajan Sangh, in those days, was a name to reckon with; it held sway over a large chunk of the public imagination.[5] The leaders of the Sangh like Arvind Buch, Shantilal Shah, Manhar Shukla, Navinchandra Barot, and so on showed up in the chawls every other day and held public meetings. Charumati Yoddha too made frequent visits to chawls. During election seasons, these leaders would be out on the hustings on full blast and throw their full weight behind the Mahajan's candidate because there was no surety that the Dalit mill workers, despite being registered members of the Mahajan, would support their candidate unconditionally and without demur. And thus, many a time, the Mahajan's candidates foundered in elections of municipal corporation and legislative assembly. But that didn't result in the Mahajan developing an animus against the hostile voters and communities, oh no.

Those were not the days, unlike today, of every house having a dedicated toilet. The chawlwallahs used public toilets whose squalid condition, in a way, reflected the destiny of those Dalit suburbs. In this context, I vividly remember Bhailal Patel, the Gandhian chairman of the municipal corporation's Health Committee, who was often seen in Rajpur at seven sharp in the morning, literally breathing down the neck of the sanitary worker on duty to clean every single corner and cranny of those reeky, soiled toilets. I don't recall if he ever recoiled in disgust or involuntarily curled up his nose while overseeing the execution of the dirty, dishonourable job.

But as I grew up, the frequency of the rounds of the Gandhians to our chawls appreciably tapered off.

The last time I saw a Gandhian activist pace up and down Dalit chawls was during the anti-reservation riots of 1981; it was Babal Mehta, the last of the thorough Gandhians whose heart was lacerated by the torn social fabric of his city. To put it bluntly, the dicey, dithering position of the Gandhians on the idea of and the movement for reservation became the root cause of their retreat not only from Rajpur but also from emergent Dalit political discourse; it was a turning point in history. A point of departure, more accurately.

The reigning sentiment in our house about Gandhi was not only one of ideological opposition but of out-and-out bitterness. From an early age, each of us kids was acquainted by Ba with Dr Babasaheb Ambedkar's life, works and views, as well as his differences with Gandhiji. All of Ba's friends were staunch Ambedkarites; the ideological climes in his mill too throbbed with Ambedkar's philosophy. Ba's friend circle included prominent Ambedkarite leaders like Rameshchandra Sandesara, Manu M. Parmar and Veeraji Bhagat who lived in our area and visited us off and on. I picked up quite a bit from their discussions about Babasaheb, Gandhiji and their fraught relationship.

Finishing primary education, I got enrolled in Class 8 in Democratic School in Gomtipur, where Dalit and non-Dalit students studied together. In the very first semester, I was introduced by my Gujarati teacher, Harendra Shastri, to the renowned Gujarati Dalit poet Chandra Parmar. Not only that, on learning that I was immensely fond of extra-curricular reading, he sent me with a recommendation letter to Anand Parmar, a prominent Dalit communist activist, who, in our very first meeting, gave me Maxim Gorky's novel *Mother* from his personal library to read. Later, he talked me through a substantial amount of communist literature. Thus, the journey of my non-curricular reading flagged off, almost by accident, with Communist-Marxist texts.

In those days, Rajpur bustled with diverse activities, initially those of the Republican Party and later, of the firebrand, rights organization Dalit Panther. Gradually, I became familiar with the leaders and Dalit poets associated with the Panther. Having devoured the libraries of Gomtipur and Rakhiyal, I went as far as

M.J. Library, hunting for books. And thus, thinkers like Ambedkar, Gandhi, Marx and Lohia began to shape my moral universe. I didn't know when and how it happened, but my intellectual capital was enriched by this early voracious reading. My elder brother, who studied at St. Xavier's College, contributed in a big way towards the development of my reading habit and the mental discipline it required. What the prolific reading of books, from personal and public libraries, did was to facilitate an early acquisition and a fine whetting of my writing and analytical skills without my knowing it.

In contemporary Dalit discourse, it is a taboo to utter a few words in favour of Gandhi even for a lay Dalit individual, to say nothing of a Dalit karmashila or a writer; so dominant and pervasive is the climate of Gandhi bashing among Dalits. There are some legitimate reasons for it, no one can deny that, but I refuse to be smothered by them. I have criticized Gandhi in no uncertain terms whenever the context justly demanded it but, at the same time, I have not turned tail whenever I've felt that Gandhi needed to be defended from trumped-up charges.

One of the principal sore points the Dalits, old and young, have with Gandhi relates to the fact that he considered untouchability a blot on Hindu religion and campaigned for its abolition, but at the same time, he explicitly endorsed the caste and *varna* systems. (He did change his views on this matter later in his life, however.) Again, he opposed the provision of separate electorates for Dalits and thwarted their social and political empowerment through the Poona Pact.

The express object of the second Round Table Conference, held in London in 1931 and attended by Gandhi and Ambedkar among other Indian leaders, was to discuss and fashion a constitutional future for India. Gandhi accepted the idea of separate electorates for Muslims and Sikhs but opposed the same being extended to Dalits. When no consensus could be arrived at, the British prime minister was authorized to take a final call on the matter. The decision went in favour of the Dalits, and Gandhiji went on a fast unto death in Yerawada Jail to protest the British government's Communal Award. Ultimately, Dr Ambedkar had to settle for a system of joint electorates with reserved seats, which led to an imposition of a dwarfish and hollow political leadership on Dalits that they haven't been able to get rid of till date. Dr Ambedkar could never forgive Gandhiji for this injustice and the Dalits today roundly curse Gandhiji for doing cruel injustice to the community.[6]

The role of the Gandhians in Gujarat during the anti-reservation riots of 1981 morphed the Dalit bitterness towards Gandhiji into an implacable and deep hatred. Following the violent riots on the issue of renaming Marathwada University after Babasaheb Ambedkar, Baba Adhav and others had constituted an Inequality Eradication Committee. A similar committee under the leadership of Bhanubhai Adhwaryu[7] had become active in Gujarat during the anti-reservation riots. (Noteworthily, the de-casted Hindus are still not able to set up anything like Jat-Pat Todak Mandal or Caste Eradication Committee in Gujarat or India.) The committee's first conference was held on 21 June 1981 at Dr Babasaheb Ambedkar Hall, where I met the eminent novelist Joseph Macwan, who was to receive the Sahitya Akademi Award for his novel, *The Stepchild*, centred on the plight of the Vankar community in rural Gujarat. In that conference, taking place amid blood-curdling riots and being attended mostly by Dalits, a people who had come under unprecedented assault from the upper castes, the question of reservation was to be discussed, and crucial resolutions around the theme were to be passed. The first resolution on the affirmative action policy was read out and thrown open for discussion. The resolution in favour of reservations had everybody's concurrence, but a Dalit youth rose to propose an amendment which sought the removal of Gandhiji's name from the resolution's preamble.

An overwhelming majority of attendees lent support to the demand of that fiery-tongued youth. On the stage were seated three eminent Gandhians – Bhanubhai Adhwaryu, Jhinabhai Desai and Dinkar Mehta. Despite their differences, the trio was essentially the product of the Gandhi Era and the furious opposition to Gandhi, voiced by the Dalit youth, was a real shocker, a veritable scorcher, to them. Ultimately, after a lot of persuasion, Gandhi's name could be retained in the resolution but not in the hearts of the dissenting Dalits, unfortunately.

Today, things have come to such a pass that one rarely encounters Gandhi's photograph in a Dalit household, especially in cities. And the Gandhians have played no small part in bringing about this sorry situation.

In 1987, when I attended the first All India Dalit Writers Conference in Hyderabad, I had heard Runoko Rashidi, the keynote speaker, spewing venom in a similar vein against Abraham Lincoln. The realization that the tragic fate of Gandhi among Dalits in India was matched by that of Lincoln among the Blacks in the US had shaken me. But it's a bitter truth and there is no escape from swallowing it. In 2001, when I happened to visit Durban to attend the World Conference against Racism, I had taken time off to go visit Phoenix Settlement. In that country, with 79 per cent of Black population, Indians/Asians constituted a tiny minority, about 2.5 per cent.[8] Among them, a vast majority was of Gujarati origin. What I learnt then about Gandhi and the Gujaratis was nothing short of an epiphany for me: Gandhi was still respected in Durban and in the whole of South Africa, but not the Gujaratis.

Phoenix, perched on a small hill surrounded by destitute Zulu settlements, was destroyed at least four times, I was told. Thc Gujarati gentleman who escorted us to the settlement was so scared that he didn't so much as step out of his expensive car throughout the visit; he just stayed put, skulking and shuddering. The manager of the settlement, a young Black man, was an ardent devotee of Gandhi. When I asked him about the Zulu attacks, he clarified, 'What do you expect them to do, if not torch the settlement whose trustees take umbrage at a stray goat or a Black person, stepping in the ashram premises for something as innocuous as a brief shelter against pouring rains? How can the Vaishnavites, Gandhi sang so highly of, be so mean?'

Thus, the reasons why the Dalits of Gujarat, in fact of the entire country, hate Gandhi are not difficult to understand. The issues of the separate electorate and the Poona Pact have progressively assumed centre stage in several Dalit movements now. The observation of 24 September, the day of signing the pact, as a Black Day too has been gaining unprecedented traction of late in Dalit circles. In his writings, speeches and talks, Dr Ambedkar preferred 'Gandhi' and 'Mr Gandhi' as terms of address for his old adversary; sometimes, he used 'Mahatmaji' but expectedly with a heavy note of sarcasm. (Gandhiji and Congress leaders addressed Babasaheb with designation like 'Bhimrao' or 'Ambedkar'.) A Dalit friend of mine, associated with the publication of Gujarati translation of Babasaheb's *What Congress and Gandhi Have Done to the Untouchables* by the state government, was unhappy about the use of 'Gandhiji' instead of plain 'Gandhi' by the translator. In this hierarchy-loving country, the idea of naming has a strange politics, one on the flip side of the politics of shaming. The use of abbreviations like Su.Jo. and U.Jo. for eminent literary figures like Suresh Joshi and Umashankar Joshi, respectively, is normal in Gujarati literary circles, but Niranjan Bhagat, a major Gujarati poet of equal stature, is addressed as Bhagat Saheb by one and all. Similarly, I think, terms like Mahatma Gandhi or Gandhiji have been in circulation for far too long for a translator to avoid, especially if they aren't thoroughly familiar with the Janus-faced politics of naming. (By the way, among the members of the Sangh Parivar, known for their stunning affability, it is customary to attach the honorific suffix 'ji' to the names of important people in public life. For example, they always say, Savarkarji, Ambedkarji, and so on. I wonder what respectable 'ji' those modest, cultured people would use for Gandhiji.)

Under such circumstances, if I say that Gandhiji helped place the Dalit question in the centre stage of India's social and political life; or that quite early on, he courageously allowed a 'Harijan' family residence in Kochrab Ashram at the risk of outraging many of his associates and endangering the financial security of the ashram; or that he created a social identity for the Dalits by coining the term 'Harijan' – I hardly receive a head-nod, let alone an endorsement from my community; not even a stray, singular voice rises in approbation. When I think or write about the provision of primary election enshrined in the Poona Pact, the Dalit scholars maintain a studied silence.

An important aspect of the Round Table Conference and Communal Award was the British government. Both Gandhi and Ambedkar had left the final decision on the matter to Ramsay MacDonald who in his imperial wisdom had decided in favour of the Dalits. However, after doing the honourable thing, when Gandhi held Ambedkar to ransom, the British government, rather than taking Ambedkar's side, turned tactically 'neutral'. How could the Dalits then and now overlook the criminal fault and chicanery of the British in that game? When I ask this question, it remains unattended and unanswered.

When I remind the Dalits, clamouring about separate electorates, of the proliferation of sub-casteism that surfaces at the time of elections and ask whether the political representation of the marginalized Dalit sub-castes, enabled by non-Dalit votes, is possible within a system of separate electorates, they don't respond, just skip the question.

The unto-death faster of Yerawada and the architect of the Poona Pact was a Sanatani Hindu to whom granting of communal award to Dalits was tantamount to partitioning the Hindu religion. To that extent, he deserves the condemnation directed at him. But the act of providing for primary election within joint electorates, the inherent lacunae in the provision notwithstanding, can certainly not be reduced to a game the cunning Bania had shrewdly rigged, as is often believed. Gandhi might have been anything – call him whatever names – but one thing he was certainly not was anti-Dalit. Oh no, never. Alas! People high on anti-Gandhi venom do not want to think of these things in a calm and coherent way.

A recent experience of the sheer madness of this antagonism. On 24 September 2018, I was invited by a Dalit friend to address a gathering on the Poona Pact at a seminar held in Sabarkantha district. Thanks for the invite, I told him, and then courteously apprised him that my take on the matter differed slightly from the conventional, calcified Dalit opinion. I could come if he was fine with it, I said. He would think about it and revert, said he. And then never did.

Once, the walls of our nondescript chawl house in Rajpur were smothered with gaudy photographs of assorted Hindu gods and goddesses. A veritable photo exhibition, a quaint art installation, if you ask me. However, all of them were gradually taken down to make room for the pictures of the Buddha and Babasaheb. Ba was extremely vigilant about a poster with Gandhi's mugshot making its way into the house, but newspapers, magazines and books were beyond the reach of his prying eyes. Thus, the ghost of Gandhi hung over our small, suburban house, to be read, condemned and even praised from time to time when no one was looking. As our family grew, we began to feel a serious space crunch, which led us to lift the ceiling and build something like a loft where people could sit and sleep. In time, the loft became the reading room and the bedroom for children, especially for Atit, my nephew, who, as the eldest child of the house, had the first and frequent dibs on that curated space. Naturally, the loft walls were colonized by the posters of the fanboy's heroes, Bruce Lee and Jackie Chan. Sometimes, I went there to read and write undisturbed. Once, I saw that there were a few photographs of Gandhi on one of the walls. This was the doing of my nephew Krunal who, I learnt, had not only stuck Gandhi alongside Lee and Chan but also bought substantial amount of literature on and by the off-limits man.

It's been years since Ba passed away. Ma too has aged considerably; she is frail now, totally dependent on others for her needs. Over years of living with me, she has begun to understand Gandhi somewhat. That apart, she saw with her own eyes how after the closure of textile mills the Dalit mill workers of Rajpur had made ends meet, not just for a few days but for years together, with the help of the Ambar Charkha,[9] the modernized, multiple-spindle upgrade of the traditional spinning wheel; it's not for nothing that eminent Gujarati writer Manubhai Pancholi, who wrote under the penname 'Darshak', described it with the epithet 'Gandhi's widow'. So, of late, Ma has stopped raising hell when I wear khadi. But her word of advice about not wearing khadi still comes to me, though from a different route. I should stay away from khadi, she says, not because I look like Gandhido, but because I look *ghaido*, a dotard, in it.

4

Creed, Conversion and Childhood

I had grown up at a very tender age. Matured prematurely, so to speak. Partly on account of the burden of responsibilities that had fallen on my kid shoulders, courtesy of our family's abject poverty. But partly also on account of my friends, a bunch of close but older friends, older to me by as much as two decades or thereabouts: writers and intellectuals like Neerav

Patel, Dalpat Chauhan, Indu Jani, Harshad Desai, and so on. Today when I have crossed fifty, I have struck intimate friendship with committed journalists and activists like Urvish Kothari, Sanjay Bhave and Jignesh Mevani, all of whom are younger to me by a couple of decades or more. God knows if having contemporaries as friends is a boon or a bane, but I have always felt that the distance in age automatically puts, even sustains, some kind of natural reserve between two people, no matter how close and candid their friendship. Bosom buddies they are, all of them, and yet, not quite.

As I think about friends, I realize with a little twinge that no friendships I had struck in school or college days have survived today, neither materially nor in memory. Except, of course, these two interfaith chums of mine, my early childhood pals, who always spring out of the black hole of my fond remembrances to give a lie to my despair. Simon Paul Gamadiya and Rahmatullah Alla Rakha Maniar. We studied in the same primary school and lived in the same ragtag suburb. Simon died young and quite tragically. Rahmatullah gave up studies mid-school and went the way, life had chosen for him; thus, we are not in touch today. But, even after all these years, their tender memories survive, as fresh and vivid as ever, like evocative engravings on the rusty plate of my mind.

In the sordid working-class chawl of Abu Kasai, bang opposite Hiralal's toilets, squatted Simon's small, modest house, though the term 'house' would be an overstatement to describe that rented low shack, known as a 'thatch' in local parlance. His was a large family that included his father Paulbhai, his mother Preetibehn[1] and six siblings, Simon being the youngest of all. Paulbhai, pronounced in the area as P + owl + bhai, was a desi Khristi[2] from Gamdi, the native village of the eminent Gujarati writer Joseph Macwan in Anand district. His forefathers, in all probability, had converted to Christianity. Preetibehn worked as a nurse in a private hospital near Lal Darwaja in Ahmedabad while Paulbhai, with his two elder brothers, worked in a textile mill.

For many kids of my age in our chawl, Simon's thatch was an address of happiness, the way a happy man's shirt was for the ailing king in the famous children's story by that title,[3] which we had read with great relish at school. By the going standards of those days, the ambience of Simon's house could safely be called modern. Very modern. He called his mother 'Mummy'. His father too was quite unlike those daunting, domineering figures we were familiar with – always keen on helping his wife with household chores: peeling and paring of vegetables, cooking a variety of dishes, dusting, mopping, and so on. Paulbhai specialized in fashioning an extremely tasty curry out of nasty, smelly veggies like gourd and bitter gourd, that too without peeling them. And what a runaway hit his fish curry was amongst the chawl people, just don't ask. 'Wanna have fish? Go for Paul's make or just drop it!' the chawl folks never tired of repeating. I wondered how the atmosphere in Simon's thatch remained ever so light and soaked in wit and humour. Much to my surprise, Simon kept his slippers on even inside the house. He and his siblings joked freely with their father, even went to the extent of slapping him on the back in jest. Everyone in Simon's house spoke 'pure' Gujarati, the sophisticated urban variety, that is. I simply marvelled at Simon's thatch, the genial air therein, the open outlook of its inhabitants towards life, and so on; for me, it had become a prototype of quintessential, supernal happiness, the presence of stinking, overflowing public toilets right in front of it notwithstanding. It didn't matter, yes, as it shouldn't.

Simon and I studied in the same municipal school. Every day, I made sure to reach his thatch half an hour, at times a full hour, in advance of the prescribed school time. The idea was to gape in admiration, even a slight envy, at Simon as he embarked on the elaborate ritual of getting ready for school at about eleven o'clock: the way he luxuriated in his long bath, scrubbing his body with a tablet of fragrant soap and washing it without stinging on bath water; the way he dried himself with a towel of his own and sprinkled a liberal quantity of talcum powder all over his body; the way he oiled his hair, put on a crisply ironed uniform and slipped a polished pair of shoes on. Would I ever get to indulge in such luxuries, I would wonder and slip into fond reveries. That the real reason behind Simon's organic happiness lay in the religious conversion his ancestors had opted for was something I realized much later in life. And that their newly embraced Christian identity made them eligible for financial assistance and other largesse from missionaries. So large and liberal was the aid, I guess, that they could give away any leftover, as expensive as a chunk of butter, to their neighbours without a second thought. Simon was perfectly healthy and fair-skinned. Average in studies, he had a dandyish streak in his personality, a kind of lady-killer air, not unnatural among boys of his age and background. He would fish out photographs of some girl, who allegedly studied in our school and whom, he said, he 'loved' like mad. Later, I realized that the girl in question was none other than Dimple Kapadia, the heroine of the superhit Bollywood flick *Bobby* (1973). Around Christmas, Simon's dusky thatch stood out in a predominantly Hindu Dalit locality, thanks to the festive look it wore, with a hanging Christmas star and all. However, for Ma and other chawl women, the distinct Christian culture of the Simons often became a point of light-hearted banter, even mockery.

The women didn't tire of reminiscing a particular episode involving Preetibehn and then died laughing. Apparently, this was how it had happened. On the day of her son David's wedding, Preetibehn set out in the chawl inviting women to formally escort the groom out of the house to lead the wedding procession. Mincing along the narrow lanes, she began to call out in her 'pure' Gujarati: '*Lo chalo mara gher. Davidne kadhavano chhe* [Come over, now. David is to be turned out of the house].' So deeply immersed she was in the Christian worldview that her language didn't have the customary vocabulary to describe the wedding ritual in question. If her language was poorer for such popular cultural terminology, I wondered if she had even heard of a term like *magbafana* that signified a ritualistic burning of a piece of dried cow-dung cake on that occasion.

A dazzlingly fair Rahmatullah stayed in a suburb called Maniarwada in Gomtipur. His abbajan worked in a mutton shop at the mouth of the same street. As his schoolmate and chum, I visited his place, a sprawling house bustling with a large family, every now and then. In those days, as I cagily picked my way through the litter of goats and hens that clogged that Muslim Street, not even a shadow of suspicion about the Muslims being different, culturally or otherwise, crossed my mind. Not for a fleeting second. I would make a beeline for his home on Eid and polish off bowls full of *sevaiya*, a sweet vermicelli pudding. Come Bakri Eid and I would eagerly look forward to the meat of Qurbani – the holy *prasad* – that Rahmatullah's father unfailingly home delivered to us every year. I have seen Rahmatullah, seen him observing *roza*s – fasts – and offering *namaz*, without being baffled or ruffled by the spectacle, as is increasingly becoming the case today.

Friendship with Simon and Rahmatullah familiarized me with the customs, culture and practices of Islam and Christianity at an early age. Resultantly, the holy message of the Bible and the Quran became an inalienable and natural part of my moral universe. Far from baulking at them, I used words like *kabrastan* and *maiyat* to refer, respectively, to graveyard and last rites, despite their diametrically different cultural significations. *Qurbani ki khalen*, the skins of animals sacrificed on Eid, were contiguous in my imagination to the hides of carcasses my people conventionally tanned. And the ideas of *urs* [celebration], *ziyarat* [pilgrimage], Santa Claus, *niyaz* [supplication], *sunnat* [circumcision], baptism and communion had an osmotic relationship in my emotional world. In fact, this mosaic of moral geography of my consciousness was a clear reflection of the material geography of my area. Beyond the western end of Dalit chawls in Rajpur lay a huddled clutch of Christian chawls which, in turn, snuggled close to the scattered bunch of Muslim ones on the periphery of a chowk opposite Mariyam Bibi's Mosque. On the eastern end lay a densely populated Muslim locality beyond which sprawled Gomtipur, a locality of upper-caste Hindus.

Looking back, I think, my close bond with Christianity, by an invisible umbilical cord, can be traced to the natal hour when I was delivered to this world by St. Mary's Nursing Home, a one-stop solution to the maternity needs of one and all in the area. Not just me, all Hindu, Muslim and Christian children of my age in the area were born there, in the gentle arms of what was popularly called Mother's Dispensary, which, as per its name, provided maternity care free of cost. Not only that, it also got the newborn babies blessed by Mother Mary at the next-door church before discharge, something which had an immense symbolic value, an ineluctable religious heft, for all the couples who approached the dispensary. So profound was the influence of Christianity among the Dalits in the area that an atheist like Ba had got a holy cross tattooed over a permanent inscription of 'Rama' on the back of his right hand. And however bizarre it might sound today, but the Dalits of Rajpur always used the term *deval*, a Gujarati equivalent of a church, to refer to local Hindu temples and shrines. Thus, the assorted deities in Hindu pantheon like Baliya Dev and Mother Maha Kali sat guiltlessly in their separate churches that we, the Hindu Dalits, visited for worship.

The church, the Christian one, had another significance too. For the young boys of the chawl, that is. The lazy louts, who kept snoring in bed until high noon on weekdays, got up early in the morning every Sunday and hung around the church gate, all spruced up and beaming. The reason for this alacrity was the clutch of cute Christian girls who came to offer prayer. The glamour boys of the chawl leered and slavered to no end as those classy girls shook hands with Christian boys of their age or hugged them. As the Mass ended, the devotees flocked to the mutton shops in the market to buy luscious provisions for their lunch, a Sunday culinary ritual they never failed to perform after prayer and communion.

I clearly remember the fanfare and the gusto with which festivals of all faiths were celebrated in Rajpur of those days. But the one that stood out in terms of the gravitational attraction it had among young men was called Natal Garba or Christmas Garba. It may sound like an oxymoron today, but the entire public road, stretching from Mariyam Bibi's chowk up to St. Josephs High School, throbbed with Christian Garba and dance performances as a part of the week-long Christmas celebrations. And not just at night, mind you, but in wintry afternoons as well. While the garba performance, staged in our chawls during Hindu festival of Navaratri, was a women-only affair, the Christmas Garba witnessed the participation both men and women. The Hindu Dalits thronged the place to watch and marvel at Christian couples swaying to the beats of garba, locking arms, cocking eyebrows and joking around and then, curse their backwardness. The crossroads of Rajpur remained aglow with fairy lights and festive mood in the run-up to the Christmas. A grand, ceremonial procession, called Natal Juloos, was taken out along those decorated roads, consisting of tinsel-bedecked trucks and open lorries, carrying Santa Claus, *bhajan* troupes and, of course, bouncy gangs of garba performers. A particularly enthusiastic Christian youth, standing atop the leading lorry, would announce on the microphone something like: 'My Hindu brothers and sisters, living in the chawls here, might not be familiar with Santa Claus. For their benefit, let me say that …'. Now, the young man mouthing these banalities, quite likely, was innocent of his Hindu ancestry, but the Dalit men and women, playing audience to him, found nothing out of ordinary in such uppity assertions. No big deal, it was.

As mentioned earlier, I had enrolled in the reputed Democratic High School for my post-primary education, though there was St. Josephs High School, popularly known as Father's School, just a stone's throw away from my home. That I couldn't study in that missionary school, set up at the centre of Dalit–Muslim localities, has always been a bit of a sore point, a lingering regret, with me. Apart from the anguish of missing out on the quality English education offered there, I particularly regretted my handicap with cursive handwriting. The popular sentiment, that the Democraticwallahs knew nothing of the cursive hand the St. Josephs-wallahs excelled at, bugged me no end; this belittling comparison, at the time, filled me with crying shame.

The Christian teachers who taught me at different schools too cast a deep impression on my mind. Mention must be made of Mother Mary-like Thresia Teacher and her polar opposite Emmanuel Sir. Thresia's house was located right at the Rajpur crossroads. Her father-in-law, a small-time businessman, went from house to house, selling ready-made garments, especially school uniforms, while her husband worked as a government officer. I still remember how, seeing that I wore the same tattered bush shirt to school every day, she had got her stingy father-in-law to part with two ready-made shirts and given them to me. Alas! Wearing clean, crisp shirts was not in my destiny. For the shirts turned out oversized, which led my elder brother to gleefully stake a claim over them and me to continue attending the school in a shirt with snot-ridden sleeves. Even in my primary school, English was taught to us by a Christian ma'am, whom we mockingly called English Teacherie. At the Democratic High School, Emmanuel was our English teacher, a Christian man who had threatened to fail me in Class 9 if I didn't take private tuition from him. Making ends meet on Ba's meagre salary was already a nightmare for our sprawling, joint family. Amid such dire financial straits, there was no way we could have spared the money for tuition and suchlike. On the day of parent–teacher meeting, when the shameless teacher put this indecent proposal to Ba, he did not resort to a litany of poverty woes, what would have been natural for a helpless man like him to do. Instead, he told the teacher coldly, his black stare boring into his face, 'Sir, I have full faith in my son's calibre. He will definitely score well in English.' And I had proved Ba right by scoring a whopping seventy out of a hundred – a lot by the standards prevailing in 1977 – without Emmanuel's tuition.

I am not very sure why we kids didn't enrol in St. Josephs High School. Perhaps, Democratic School had a better academic reputation, or it may have been just a case of social respectability and conspicuous consumption. However, later with the visible downfall in the quality of education at the Democratic and in view of my weak, wobbly English, Ba had resolved to enrol Atit, the son of my elder sister, in a missionary school for primary education. To ensure that Atit got admitted in schools like St. Aloysius or Happy Home right from the nursery stage, a burnt-fingered Ba had made meticulous plans since the boy's toddler days. He had a friend called Damas in the mill he worked at. The man, whose Hindu name was Dahyo, was involved proactively in the assorted missionary activities and programmes organized by the Jesuit church. With his astute finger on his friend's pulse, Ba managed somehow – pinching a penny here, skipping a meal there – to give Damas a rupee or two every month as donation to the mission, just to ensure that Atit got enrolled in the missionary school through his good offices. When Atit turned three and Ba broached the subject of his enrolment, Damas began to hum and haw and later, when confronted directly, simply dodged the issue. The result – Atit couldn't be enrolled in a missionary school. After that, whenever Damas visited us, Ba made it a point to address him deprecatingly as Dahyo, taking him down from his exalted religious identity.

I have heard and read a lot about the aggressive proselytization effort of the missionaries in India. Today, when I hear the supremo of the Rashtriya Swayamsevak Sangh (RSS), a far-right extremist organization, brand Mother Teresa's well-meaning welfare activities as camouflaged proselytization effort, my agonized mind races back to the late 1970s and early 1980s, when my writing career had experienced its first flowering and eventual flourishing. The first of my articles in print with a formal byline was on Mother Teresa and it was a denominational, upper-caste Hindu magazine called *Audichya Samachar*, mind you, edited by one of my Brahmin teachers, which had published it. He had encouraged me to write that article, an article on Mother Teresa penned by a Dalit boy and published in a Brahmin magazine. Period.

A similar, somewhat confounding memory goes back to the day when for the first time my photograph had appeared in print. Not in a Dalit magazine, but in *Sadhana*, a magazine of the RSS. The occasion was Ambedkar Vandana Rally, organized at Sarangpur Circle in Ahmedabad by the Akhil Bhartiya Vidyarthi Parishad (ABVP), the youth wing of the RSS, on 14 April to pay homage to Dr Bhimrao Ambedkar on his birth anniversary. The rally was flagged off by Jetha Parmar, the first ever Dalit mayor of Ahmedabad from the Indian National Congress (INC). The editor of *Sadhana*, Vishnu Pandya, had pushed and stationed me – a curious, clueless spectator – in the line of ABVP's student–activists, standing near Dr Ambedkar's bust at the photo-op moment. Later, the report of the event had appeared in the magazine with the photograph, sporting a slightly dazed yours truly in the first row. It sounds like a pipe dream today, a Dalit student penning an essay on Mother Teresa for a Brahmin mouthpiece or an INC mayor flagging off ABVP's rally. But not long ago, this was an everyday sociopolitical reality of this country. Yes, it was.

In the current climate of hysteria surrounding conversion and *ghar wapasi*, the return of the prodigal converted son to the Hindu fold, I wish to speak categorically about and place on record one thing. Which is, of the five to ten families in our chawl, which regularly received assistance in cash or in kind from the missionaries, not a single person, let alone an entire family, has converted to Christianity till date. On the contrary, I am aware of so many Christians from the chawls who had compulsively reassumed their Hindu names, surnames and identity, either openly or on the sly. One such family, whose proverbial homecoming has happened, is my immediate neighbour here in Gandhinagar and when Ma addresses them with their Christian names, I can clearly see their discomfiture; they feel odd, very odd.

Thus, going by my personal experiences in Rajpur and surrounding areas, the idea that the missionary's real intent behind service and assistance is religious conversion just does not hold water; it is an utterly spurious notion. At the same time, unfortunately, I haven't seen the missionary's axiomatic kindness break its boundaries and grow into a broad-based struggle for the human rights of Dalits or indigent non-Dalits, when they are violated.[4] When Simon dropped out of school and joined Pilot Dairy as a daily wager, he was accused of stealing a milk can by the dairy owners. The police brutalized him, thrashed him black and blue, and then, after a week of excruciating pain and suffering, Simon died. And yet the inhuman torture and eventual death of Simon didn't become a matter worth a protest, neither for the Dalits nor for the Christian missionaries. The thatch Simon's family lived in had a horizontal room and a small veranda perpendicular to it. With the implementation of a Town Planning Scheme in Rajpur, a part of the veranda went into the state's land pooling and readjustment drive for building public infrastructure.

However, the land deduction the thatch suffered was not good enough in the eyes of the government for the compensatory allotment of a house to Simon's family in the slum quarters, built for the displaced. To make things worse, their landlord Mahiji, the old fart, sold the thatch along with his house and fled. The new landlord was not willing to rent the thatch to Simon's family. Ultimately, they had to leave the place with a heavy heart and dripping eyes. Battered and shattered to smithereens, Simon's family survived somehow, but not in one piece, and my childhood dream of a happy home wilted prematurely, died a painful death by the time I crossed the threshold of youth.

The dream of writing in a flowing, cursive hand and speaking flawless, fluent English too couldn't be realized due to the missed opportunity of going to St. Josephs. But the fact that my elder brother eventually graduated with a major in English from the prestigious St. Xavier's College in Ahmedabad and opened a brave new world of books and ideas for all of us is a consolation. Certainly, and a big one.

5

Soak Me Through, Damn You!

Crazy rains crashed down outside. I was inside, celebrating with friends the arrival of monsoon with cups of tea and plates of freshly fried, spicy *gota* in the canteen of the state secretariat, Gandhinagar. The city had turned lush green. The atmosphere was pleasantly humid, cool and fragrant. Over sips of tea and bites of pakoras, my friends had turned ecstatic, mouthing cliches like, 'What a lovely season! I feel like writing a poem.' In their high, they went a step too far and asked me, 'Why Chandu! The monsoon is your favourite season too, isn't it?'

And I get transported to the chawls of Rajpur, soaked in the endless days of monsoon.

As soon as the beating heat of summer let up somewhat, the new semester in schools kicked off, stained clouds began to scud in the skies and intimations of the monsoon knocked on the door, we, the Maherias, would swing into action to welcome the rains in our modest chawl home – in a different vein, though. On the auspicious day of Akshaya Tritiya, a farmer might stand in his furrowed fields and look expectantly at the shining skies, the shelf of his hand shielding his eyes, but we, like the families of Dalits and labourers all around, would make a beeline for the Prem Darwaja market in Ahmedabad to buy *miniyu*, a sheet of cheap tarpaulin, to cover our rusted, perforated tin-sheet roof so that the lovely rain didn't make its way inside the house. On a Sunday or a weekday after office hours, depending upon the urgency of the situation, Ba would go to the market, one of us brothers in tow, purchase a big, blue miniyu and get us to spread it on the roof. The house-tops of all chawls in those days sported either neatly laid, desi roof-tiles or corrugated tin sheets. In case of the former, the tiles would be re-laid while the latter resorted to the trick of miniyu. Throughout the monsoon, the rooftops of all the chawls in Ahmedabad sported a cover of protective sheets, plastic or tarpaulin, and a litter of stones and bricks pinning them down. That was our way of welcoming rains, the begetter of problems, troubles and even catastrophes. Not with gota, glee and gaiety.

Miniyu was just one part of the preparation, though. Another headache was protecting the sawdust we used as fuel in sigri. We ensured that the huge jute bags, bulging with sawdust, were carefully shrink-wrapped before the first showers. For, God forbid, if moisture got to the bags, the whole exercise of cooking would turn into a nightmare. When the downpour continued for days together, we ran out of flour. In those days of labouring, buying essentials and surviving on day-to-day basis, the idea of stocking grains and stuff was just unimaginable. Another welcoming ritual involved taking out all the furniture of the house and spraying the now-banned DDT in liberal measure all over the place to ward off mosquitoes and other infectious bugs. And yet, year after year, our monsoon flowed over with squalor, mosquitoes and malaria. Of the forty-odd years of my life in the chawl, hardly a year went by when I didn't catch the malaria bug.

Located at the mouth of the chawl, my house had the luxury of having the footpath for its extended veranda. The lean peepul tree on the footpath, an add-on to the luxury, made our scorching summer afternoons and suffocating nights bearable through its shade and susurrating breeze, respectively. That squat, small house of ours evidently couldn't accommodate a sprawling family, so almost half of the family had to make the footpath its home. Except, of course, for the days of bone-chilling cold and pouring rain. Thus, I have spent about half of my life on the footpath, and quite happily at that. Barring those days, when the downpour didn't allow you to sleep outside and the suffocating, hot humidity made life impossible inside. The luxury of a ceiling fan was still a few years away. So, as soon as the rains let up and the eaves stopped dripping, we, the squatters, would rush outside. Ba and a couple of us brothers would crouch beneath an overhang of tin sheet, drawing makeshift curtains on three sides. The conditions of living were wretched indeed, but they were common to all, the Dalits and the working-class people living in chawls. And wretched they are, even today. But we were lucky in that we had the whole of the footpath to ourselves, a comfort others couldn't but envy.

Megh Raja, the Lord of Rains, then was not so miserly as now. Not a stingy type, he just let loose, came down with all his might on the miniyu. The poor thing, though pinned by weighty bricks, wouldn't hold out for long. And the roof would start dripping. Here and there and everywhere. A battery of bowls and buckets would be placed strategically on the floor to catch the drips. Sitting in a corner, hugging my folded knees, I would pass the day watching the drip feeding the scowling bowls, but the nights turned taxing and long.

Our house had a single door and no windows. So, barring the spells of wet days, the sunroof of our house – a tin sheet, basically – remained open throughout the year. Our natural air conditioner, that. At the slightest inkling of showers, a hue and cry would go up, 'Hey, close the top! Run, run!' Sometimes, in the hubbub and hurry, the tin sheet would get so tightly lodged that it became impossible to throw it open again, leaving us in damp dark for days on end.

During *chomasu*, the four months of rains, I don't recall having ever seen any of my kin floating paper boats on rivers of logged rainwater or marvelling at the beauty of rainbow arching the sky or getting excited by the first showers. The image from those days, rivetted on my mind, is that of my mother instead, a terrified woman, fright written all over her face, muttering the name of our family goddess for mercy. That haunting image doesn't let me relish rains even today. More than the rain-god, it was Varuna, the god-sovereign, the ruler of the sky, that Ma was scared stiff of. Rains, accompanied by blustery wind and thunderbolts, would spook her, and with an involuntary shudder, she would break into loud chanting of 'O my holy Mother!' This urgent, exquisite prayer urged Varuna to go soft on the roof of her house so that it didn't grow wings and take off. A little bribe too would be discreetly slipped in. 'I would make an offering,' she would tell Varuna secretly 'of a plateful of *bundi* laddu in the month of Bhadarvo if you spared my house.' And she kept her word without fail. The reason I like bundi laddu so much, thus, can be traced to the little scam Ma pulled on Varuna and the booty of God's share of laddus she brought home as prasad for us kids.

During monsoon, the chawls of Rajpur became ground zero for casualties and calamities like collapsing of walls, roofs being blown off, electrocution, rainwater flooding the houses and streets, etc. The municipal school across the road just needed an excuse of showers, however scant and light, to turn into an island. And so was the case with our house. Leaving or entering it entailed wading into knee-deep, at times chest-high, swathes of heaving, dirty water. Going to work in deluge days became a real ordeal. Even today, I shudder to think of that night when, on my way home from Maninagar railway station,

I had been swept away by the huge whoosh of rainwater in the Kankaria Yard and almost drowned. Just last year, learning that Ma had suddenly taken ill, I had rushed to Rajpur. And the way Ahmedabad, the so-called smart city of touted Vibrant Gujarat, had confronted me with the challenge of negotiating waterlogged roads and streets, just don't ask. Today, when I utter stuff like I don't like monsoon or the prospect of getting wet in rain, my audience gasps, their eyebrows raised in mock surprise. How could someone, who has spent most of his life's monsoons in just two pairs of mostly wet clothes, still like to get soaked is a question beyond them, one they don't have the necessary bandwidth to process. Again, using toilets in those soggy days was tantamount to scaling the ladder to heaven, nay to hell, to be fair to the public toilets that overflowed with grime and excreta. Off went all the lovely songs for a rainy day one learnt in pre-primary classroom, as one stepped up to those reeky things. What remained was an oppressive sense of nausea and disgust.

And what to say of the festivals that fell during the monsoon; they have their own oddly unique stories to tell. The first festival to fall in the very first month of chomasu is Lord Jagannath's Ratha Yatra, a chariot festival celebrated on the second day of the month of Ashadh. I haven't missed a single one of them, the grand processions they take out, in my childhood and adolescent years. Like Lord Ranachodrai, the presiding deity of the procession, I too had my mama's home in the area called Saraspur. Bhawan Mama stayed in the railway colony in Saraspur, so on the day of Ratha Yatra, all of us would pitch camp there from early morning to late in the night. The spectacular holy chariots of Lord Jagannath, his brother Balabhadra and his sister Subhadra, pulled by rows of devotees and members of Khalashi community with the help of thick ropes, would halt at Saraspur on their way up and down, and none of us would miss this double delight for the world. The now-iconic, huge Ambedkar Hall was under construction then. The supernal joy I had of watching the procession, perched atop its half-erected walls and pillars, has been unparalleled, unmatched even by the delight of presiding over public meetings, held there.

The month following Ashadh, i.e., Shravan, was then, as now, considered auspicious, a month of fasting, vows and *tapa*. But my memories of Shravan revolve only around the month-long community reading of the Mahabharata in the veranda of the harridan Nathi's house, bang opposite mine. I faintly remember even getting inspired and reading a couple of chapters from the epic during the holy month. For the people of the chawl, it was not really the epic but the saucerful of tea, served to the audience around midnight, that pulled them like magnet to the recounting of the epic tale. It may be customary these days for hip audience to approach the hall-katha, all shining and spruced-up, but in case of our chawl-katha, men showed up in loin-clothes and tattered vests or were just plain naked above the waist. And what about a lamp of ghee, incense sticks, camphor burning, you ask, eh? All I recall is that the atmosphere in the veranda turned redolent with the tired wind those poor, labouring Dalits, sitting on their haunches, broke every now and then.

The other two major monsoon festivals we celebrated were Raksha Bandhan and Janmashtami. Regarding the former, what I remember more vividly than the now-prevalent fad of a sister tying a fancy rakhi on her brother's wrist is the custom of a Brahmin forcing his way into a Dalit household, tying a rakhi and making the family cough up two rupees in *dakshina*, a form of ritual extortion. A gang of around ten to twelve Brahmins, who lived in the chawls around, rightfully went on a rampage throughout the area, but in our case, sadly, a priest from our native village too paid a special swindling visit and made life difficult. When that pot-bellied plunderer popped off, it was his son-in-law and the latter's father that took turns year after year paying unsolicited visits, continuing the tradition of fleecing. Theirs was a well-to-do family, and if Ma was to be believed, the father was a manager at some talkies in Ahmedabad. But how could he have allowed a little thing like that to stand between himself and the enormous fortune he stood to make in one day? The family's fair complexion, pure speech and superior financial status made it incumbent upon Ma to offer a bigger dakshina than our strained circumstances could afford.

In Rajpur, the birth of Lord Krishna at the stroke of midnight of Janmashtami was not celebrated by firing crackers, as is the case today. We deployed our congenital faculty of jugaad to wish happy birthday to the god in a uniquely innovative way that would put the raucous, rumbling tunes a DJ spins these days to shame. The young men of the chawl would tie a small metal sheet or a lota and suchlike at the back of their bicycles, most of them on rent, and then wheel up and down the main road, announcing through an orgy of sharp rattles the birth of the god to the whole harried world.

I have known water intimately, both in shortage and superfluity. Today I live in my house in the state capital with a plenitude of water – there is water here to use, to store and to waste. In those days, our chawl had just one public tap, shared by about twenty-odd households for their day-to-day and festive requirements. Again, the water supply was erratic and restricted to just three hours a day. Even then, thanks to the trousseau of troubles the monsoon brought, my child mind would curse the rains throughout the four soggy months, 'Why do you pour down here in

Ahmedabad? What do you think, damn you, that people in this space-crunched city want to till the land, reap a harvest?' I have had occasions in my life to see drought and its ravages at close quarters. That apart, quite a few literary texts I read have had gut-wrenching descriptions of famine. Dilip Ranpura's novel *Teary Light* is a case in point where a dying girl, who has never seen monsoon in her short life, asks her parents what rain looks and feels like. Overwhelmed, her parents fulfil the last wish of their daughter by sprinkling some water on her face. 'Look, my dear! That's how rain feels,' they say, their voice choked with grief. The episode moistens my eyes every time I read it. In 2015, when I was posted in Dhoraji, I was puzzled by the orgy of fireworks accompanying heavy rains in the sky. Upon enquiry, I was told that people were celebrating the likely overflowing of the dam on the Bhadar with the first rains of the season looking so promising. A good monsoon would ease their water woes throughout the year, a people who knew thirst thought. That was when I exquisitely realized just how important monsoon can be in people's life.

Despite all this, the years of monsoon-spawned distress have driven me to develop a kind of cold dislike for the season. Quite a few of the Dalit houses in Rajpur's chawls have become pucca over the years, and public amenities too have improved in the area somewhat. But the insane waterlogging, the swampy bogs and the cave-ins on the main and internal roads have refused to leave Rajpur and the wretched lives of its residents.

After Bhadarvo was done with its demented downpour, the season of gloom and grey would finally ease its way into the burnished bright of Aso, the month that heralds the festive season of Diwali. And yet, the dark memories of dreadful monsoon would rankle with people long after. Cent per cent rains may warm the cockles of a farmer's heart and a good monsoon might give policymakers the hope for a flourishing economy, but for us poor, quite predictably, the rains have become synonymous with hassle, hardships and horror, nothing else.

In a scorching afternoon of May 2014, I was wandering in Ramgiri, a mountain in central India from where

Yaksha, the demi-god and lovelorn protagonist of Kalidasa's epic *Meghadoota*, had sent a message to his beloved based in Alakapuri through a dark, northward-bound cloud. I don't know what message I would send to Varsharani, the rain-queen, if a heavy, moisture-laden cloud agrees to become my messenger. Do you?

6

A Diwali No Less, That

The last month in the calendar according to Vikram Samvat is called Aso and the no-moon night of Aso is celebrated as Diwali. Ma's pet proverb about the festival went like, 'Nine days of Navratri, the tenth is Dussehra, and the twentieth is Diwali.'

In the last five decades, our family has celebrated the annual festive season, almost all of them, in our small tin-shed house in the chawl of Abu Kasai. It's been two decades since I moved to this dull governmental city called Gandhinagar, in a house that can be described at the most as my probationary home. For, as soon as Diwali approaches, I make a beeline, as an auto-response to a default setting, for my ancestral home in Rajpur.

The Diwali of my childhood flagged off immediately after the Navratri, a nine-night-long festival of garba performance and worship of holy Mother Amba. Ba's weekdays passed in sweat and toil at a Rakhiyal-based mill that manufactured fabric for vests and frocks. But as the chawl warmed up to the intimations of Diwali, he would know it was time to swing into action. On a Saturday evening, he would take an old earthen pot, fill it half with hydraulic lime and pour water in it, just enough to soak the lime thoroughly. The mixing of the lime with water would set off a vigorous chemical reaction, causing the mixture to boil up. After a while, the plumes of fume would subside, and the pot would be left undisturbed overnight. Next morning, the solution of slaked lime would be used to whitewash the stained and flaking walls with a thick, heavy brush, and with that, our Diwali celebrations would kick in.

Our house was just a four-wall business, a dingy hovel without windows or ventilation. Nothing more than that. I know, it's difficult today to imagine a house in posh urban societies and gated colonies without a gallery or a sprawling balcony. However, with a little effort and a visit to a working-class suburb or a slum in Ahmedabad, one would surely be able not just to imagine but also confirm that half of the city still dwells in homes without windows.

The long, unrelenting spell of monsoon rains would have ended finally to everyone's relief, but its presence would still be felt indoors in the form of fusty odour, hanging in the air. Something had to be done about that. Coats of white on walls, thus, served a dual purpose: dispelling the settled mould and upholding the promise of renewal Diwali brought. On the day of whitewashing, everybody got up a couple of hours earlier than usual. First of all, the whole ever-prospering world of clutter, preserved between the roof of corrugated iron sheet and wooden floor of the loft, would be taken down. That assorted junk of old earthen pots, China-clay pickle jars, broken legs of string cots, old utensils, torn clothes, broken metal trunks and a host of dusty sackcloth bundles. Then all of it, the flotsam and jetsam of Dalit life, would be dusted thoroughly and wiped with a wet cloth before it was consigned back to where it belonged in deference to the tacit rule of non-discardment, which said, 'Everything, even a stored snake, has its use.'

Once the matter of scraping was settled, everyone would start scrubbing the walls, with sandpaper if available or with any abrasive material at hand. Evidently, the exercise demanded strenuous physical labour, and with my malnourished body, I could stake no claim to the task. Everyone at home, not just my siblings but even my parents, mockingly called me a 'corpse', a dysphemism for a weakling, and thus, avoided pointing out to me a job involving severe strain or substantial effort. However, spreading a carpet of sand on the floor as a protection against lime-water stains on the slate-stone tiles and the daub of cow dung was my responsibility. I would go to the plot of government-owned wasteland nearby, one that we curiously called a 'farm', bring over sand in a bucket or a large metal plate and sprinkle handfuls of it all over the floor. Then Ba and my brothers would get down to business. In principle, the project execution was a team effort, but the lion's share of work would be done single-handedly by Ramanbhai, who worked tirelessly like an old hand, treating the wall as a wide canvas, painting it in broad strokes. Thanks to his speed and finesse, the whole drawing room, the biggest room in the house, would be taken care of by the afternoon. That day, we would invariably have khichdi for lunch, the fast food of the poor, which everyone swallowed down in great hurry and returned to work, now of putting the furniture back in place. A scintillating room and a bright veranda would conjure up a mirage before our eyes, of a gently shimmering Diwali showing up at our door.

In days following the weekend, Ramanbhai would paint the doors, the roadside grille, and so on. In those days, my kid-eyes had got accustomed to just one colour, a dismal brick red in which the doors and the grille were painted year after year. The colour of train coaches. The history of this monochromatic obsession goes back to the largess of Bhawan Mama who worked in the Indian Railways as a gangman. Once when he visited us, he had brought along a full container of oil paint, which the Indian Railways, done with coating its train coaches, had to spare. The big paint haul had lasted us a couple of Diwalis, but after that the shade stuck to our minds. Thus, every Diwali, as we set about procuring paint for doors and grille, we couldn't but settle for the brick red.

The preparatory chores specific to Diwali, like whitewashing, painting and house-cleaning, went on and on until the last moment. Women did all Diwali chores – scrubbing brass utensils, washing bedsheets, quilts, and so on – in the three-hour window when water was available in the public tap. The framed photographs of gods, goddesses, the Buddha and Babasaheb would be taken off the walls for dusting and wiping, and hung back as the glint in their protective glass informed the beholders' admiring eyes. The wooden shelves installed on walls would flaunt a shiny line of brass and copper utensils, freshly burnished with lemon peels and ripe tamarind fingers. And thus, the entire house would be reborn, delivered from the womb of Diwali in mint condition.

In those days of abject poverty and utter privations, the only Diwali shopping spree we could go on, however grudgingly, was the purchase of modest, ready-made garments for the family minus Ba and Ma. The fixing of the shopping day depended upon the day Ba got Diwali bonus from the mill's management. However, uncertainty of time notwithstanding, no one nursed any doubts about the shopping destination: the ready-made garment shop of Bachubhai near Tran Darwaja in Ahmedabad, a one-stop solution to the material needs of the entire labour class of Ahmedabad, a place of pilgrimage for purchase. Ba would disrobe us on the municipality's footpath outside the shop, a public trial room where we stood stark naked without blushing and make us fight our way into pairs of new shorts or trousers to arrive at the exact size of the garments to be bought. Only then did the shopping begin.

The festival season started with Dhanteras, a day that marked the formal beginning of Diwali with a ritual worship of Lakshmi, the goddess of wealth and prosperity. Having grown up in an affluent family, Ma had brought along, we heard on the grapevine, a veritable bounty of gold and silver ornaments in her trousseau. But as our family grew and education of us kids took off, Ma's jewellery too grew wings and took off one by one from her person and from her safe. One thing that surprised me no end back then was the dazzling profusion of jewellery shops in a poor, working-class suburb like Rajpur, such that they outnumbered those dealing in groceries and toiletries. Such that the inaugural issue of *Dalit Panther* had carried an advertisement of a jewellery shop, quite bizarrely, amidst pages proclaiming 'Halla Bol' against capitalism, exploitation, and so on. Growing up, I realized that those shops dealt neither in making nor selling of ornaments but in credit extending. A bunch of moneylenders, those goldsmiths. So, after reckless bouts of selling and pawning her jewellery over years, the only *dhan* Ma was left with was a nose ring and a pair of bangle-like anklets, our family's ostensible wealth to appease Mother Lakshmi with. While pleading with the goddess for wealth and happiness, Ma would go around the house sprinkling the auspicious *kanku* water everywhere, especially on our school texts and notebooks.

Next day, the day of Kali Chaudas, Ba would return from work with paper-cones, carrying half a kilo each of *chavanu*, *ganthia* and *sev* from the mill's canteen. There would also be a box of sweets, mostly *mohanthal*, to go with the savoury snack mix. This was all we had for Diwali, the stuff that spelt and sussed out Diwali for us. And yet, in the days following the issuance of bonus, the air in Rajpur would be shot through with the throb and thrill of the festival. The area underwent a pampering makeover. The suburban roads witnessed an overnight doubling of drunkards, swaying and tottering their way to nowhere, as a fleet of hawkers selling liver, belly and kebabs in open handcarts stank out the place. All houses in the chawls, as a rule, put on a decorative, festive look, but the ones with electricity connection beamed up with colourful string lights and bulbs. Festoons of glitzy papers and tinsels on doors and entrances welcomed the festival of renewal with their dancing dazzle and swaying shimmer. Curiously enough, even in those chawls, the icons of sordid poverty, Diwali celebration had a distinctive class character; the rich made a spectacle out of it for the poor to gape and grumble at.

On the eve of Diwali, Ma would chop sugarcane stalks to make portable torches out of them and recount the history behind the ritual to us. After the fourteen-year exile in the forest, when King Rama came back to Ayodhya on the eve of Diwali, the people welcomed him back with small burning torches like these, she would say, pointing out the mermeraya in front of her. The tradition of lighting these makeshift torches on the night of Diwali has continued since then, she would add, beaming. The chawls had extended that tradition by adding to it the ritual of firing crackers and dumping the resulting debris in the chowk (actually on the concrete slab over the septic tank near Hiralal's toilets).

Thanks to the grinding penury, I had to torch my desire to fire crackers year after year. (However, Ma had a self-righteous version to trade to the neighbours, 'Our kids don't crave that kind of indulgence, oh no.') But I still remember how crackers going off outside made our Diwali inside truly unforgettable. A lingering scarcity of resources precluded us from applying for an electricity connection until 1978 and, thus, we solely depended on a desi lantern for all purposes, be it Diwali celebration or nocturnal studying. Every year, as Diwali approached, we would ensure that we had chimneys to spare, at least three to four, to last us the festive season. For as soon as a bomb blasted outside our house, the chimney of our lantern cracked. Ostensibly, Diwali is a festival of lights, but I had to spend quite a few of them in darkness either because the lantern conked out or because we ran out of all spare chimneys. Quite a few of pitch-dark Diwali nights wore on like that, with us kids falling asleep, waiting for the dawn of Gujarati New Year to break.

But the New Year's dawn, most of the time, came with a promise of disasters than hope. Early in the morning, everyone would purchase *sabaras*, auspicious salt crystals, from small-time hawkers, mostly young lads who came to sell luck to a people who set much store by it. Then, everyone would hang festoons made from sacred leaves of ashoka tree over doors, and ritually discard old earthen water pots and suchlike. Ma and other women of the neighbourhood would take old pots, cracked earthenware and other detritus from their homes, march out together, muttering a fervent plea, 'Let the sickness of all kinds leave my home and take a plunge into the black sea …' and dump it near the toilets. The Diwali revellers on the road outside would plead with them for an old pot or an odd bowl to fire crackers from inside them. As the bombs, set to fire and tucked quickly under overturned vessels, went off, the earthen shards would fly all around and rain down on the tin-sheet roof of our house with a loud, metallic clatter. At times, the shattering clang overhead would chime with the cracking chimney of a lone, lugubrious lantern, consigning the house to the reign of darkness. The dump of the mermeraya and the debris of the earthenware would invariably clog the chamber pots, or the septic tank attached to the toilets, forcing us to welcome the sunrise of the New Year with a rank smell of urine and excreta overflowing from the toilets.

We began our New Year day, almost as a habit, not with sweets or some such stuff but with a cup of tea. Quite often, it so happened that, of all goddamn days, we wouldn't get the supply of milk on the most auspicious day. What luck! Mind you, those were the days when the celebrated milk revolution, to be carried out later by Verghese Kurien, didn't exist even as a concept. Unlike today, milk was not an easily available commodity, something that you could purchase over the counter when the mood got you. It was available only at the municipality's official outlet, a single distribution centre that twenty chawls of the area, including ours, hopelessly depended on. The early risers, the overcautious and the fixated lot would reserve their places in the ever-lengthening and never-ending queue for the milk supply; after standing for hours in the line, people at the end of their tethers took it out on the fellow buyers in the form of an exchange of arguments, expletives and blows. On such occasions, the entrenched caste hierarchy among the Dalits would reassert itself, egging the Vankar majority to ride roughshod over us, a minority of lowly chanotara. Ma, the poor thing, would stand in the line for hours together, cursing the cunning vendor, the greedy customers and her blasted lot and at the end of it all, come back home, empty-handed and frustrated.

Unfazed by the tsunami of troubles flooding upon her – the Ganga of the gutter spillage, flowing along the face of our house, the milk woes, the chimney distress and the roof litter – Ma would get us ready, all bathed and beaming in the ready-made clothes from Bachubhai's, for a visit to the ancient temple of Lord Ranchhodrai in Gomtipur. For her, this was a proper ritual to inaugurate the New Year with. No excuses or arguments about it. Ba, a sworn atheist who loathed such visits, would join us too so as not to be a spoilsport on a day when everybody was in high spirits, though for different reasons. I still remember one such visit, sadly the last in the series Ba had made willy-nilly so as not to hurt Ma's feelings.

At the crack of dawn, Ba, mini-me in his arms, waited in the heaving crowd of devotees for our turn to have *darshan* of Lord Ranchhodrai. Just when we were about to make it, the sentry brought down the bamboo pole blocking our entry. Ba's tummy and my legs were pressed against the pole as the crazy crowd pushed and crushed us from behind. My loud, scared weeping and Ba's muffled groans were lost in the echoes of collective chants, 'Victory to Ranchhod.' Nobody gave a damn. The episode turned out to be an epiphany for Ba, a one-to-one face off, not with Lord Ranchhod, but with a disaster. After that real brush with death, Ba didn't visit a temple ever again, though Ma's rounds continued unabated.

The customary temple visit would be followed by the most awaited event of the Gujarati New Year, a feast of a plateful of chavanu and a chunk of mohanthal. Strutting around in chawls in new clothes, meeting friends and comparing their clothes with ours etc., would go on until afternoon. Ma would lovingly cook a curry of luffa mixed with black-eyed peas and khichdi for lunch that day, believing that the fibres of luffa would bestow health upon the diners through the year.

For the rest of the city, the New Year of Vikram Samvat may well begin with sunrise, but for the working-class Dalits of Rajpur, it dawned in real earnest only at night, a rural tradition we had brought along to the city. A tradition in which one laboured through the day, be it Diwali or New Year, and celebrated through the night. Thus, during the New Year day, the chawlwallahs crossed, met and even spoke to one another maybe a hundred times, but formal greetings were not exchanged any time before the night. In those days, the expressions that have become common today, like 'Happy New Year' and 'Saal Mubarak', were alien to us. All we knew and said in greeting was 'Jesikrasna', a local condensation of 'Jai Shree Krishna'. We even didn't know that elders had to be greeted with prostration and people of same age by a handshake; we were not so 'cultured'. Whoever we ran into would be greeted with a mechanical muttering of 'Jesikrasna'. Today, I am so much at a loss for words when I think about those times in which we kids addressed all the chawl elders by their first names, that too in singular. Thus, I don't remember having addressed elderly people with familial honorifics like Bhai, Kaka,

Mama or Mota; we called, for example, the seniors of the chawl as Morar Master, Balo Dhedh, Ramo Fitter, Harakho, Mahiji, Khushal, Keshav, and so on. And the same went for the women ... The terms of endearment and respect, like Kaki, Mami, Foi and Bhabhi, were neither known nor used. Despite such informality and a certain immediacy of social interaction, our hearts surged with warmth and fellow feeling that is increasingly on the wane these days. That old habit of informal, interpersonal address died hard, but I wonder if it really required to die in the first place.

All these festive preliminaries notwithstanding, the Diwali celebration, in the true sense of the term, began only towards the end of the festive season, on the evening of the Bhai Bij, when we tagged along with Ma to Mama's place. Mama's sons worked in textile mills and, thus, by the standards of those days, their family was deemed well-to-do. Of his many sisters, only Ma lived in Ahmedabad and came visiting on Bhai Bij, a day that celebrated the bond of love between a brother and a sister. So, we received a royal welcome and special treatment at Mama's. His sons and daughters would be on their toes, looking after us and treating us to sweets, delicacies, etc., until we were full and could have no more. At the time of bidding goodbye, Ma would get a saree and a utensil, and we kids hard cash as Diwali gifts, something that gave us the real Diwali zing.

However old I may get, I won't be able to erase a few Diwalis from the slate of my memory, so deeply etched have they been on my mind for good, gleeful and gory reasons. First, the Diwali in 1969, the year of horrifying communal riots that held Ahmedabad in its vice-like grip. For months, the city was under curfew. The flames of communal hatred leapt so high, and the lamp of humanity burnt so low that people increasingly felt it impossible to inhabit the city. Reading the precarity of the times, Ma had moved us to her parents' place in Chhimpadi village in Kheda district. I won't ever forget the Diwali I celebrated that year in my *mosal*, the place of maternal grandparents, the only Diwali I celebrated out of Rajpur and without my parents. (I wouldn't visit my mosal ever again.) As Diwali approached that year, Ma had briefly come over to give us Diwali gifts: a pair of new clothes and some snacks. The Dalit Street in Chhimpadi then had no more than five to seven houses; everything looked hopelessly dreary and dismal, forget about the festive mood. On the night of Diwali, Mama had taken us to the house of the village Darbar[1] for begging. Holding his dented begging bowl before the Garasiya woman, Khushalmama had pleaded in the meekest possible tone, 'Sister, he is my nephew, has come all the way from Ahmedabad, please give some more today.' That night, we had celebrated Diwali on alms. Next day, donning new clothes, we had kept knocking about for a few hours in the street, clueless about where else to go and what else to do until the afternoon.

The second unforgettable Diwali of my life dated back to 1971–72, the year of the India–Pakistan war and the birth of Bangladesh. As a part of the National Service Scheme (NSS) team of St. Xavier's College, Ahmedabad, my elder brother had gone to some city in West Bengal to serve the refugees from Bangladesh. To ensure that his family didn't miss him on Diwali, my touring brother had made a clever arrangement: The gang of his Brahmin–Bania friends would visit us in the chawl on the New Year day to cheer us up. Really? Well, the prospect of English-educated young men from the monied class visiting us at our humble home in the chawl warranted befitting 'special' arrangements for their convenience. The only pair of chairs and table in the chawl, proudly possessed by Devo lathho, were borrowed and placed right in the middle of the living room. That apart, four to five ramshackle chairs and wobbling stools, practically begged from a few reluctant neighbours, were laid down for serving snacks and tea. No doubt, the Savarna friends of Motabhai spoke to us with love and affection and sat for quite long, trying to amuse us. That Diwali, what we felt most grievously about, however, was neither Motabhai's absence nor the presence of his funky friends, filling in for him, but the feast of chavanu and sweets that we so unwillingly had to sacrifice.

The third memorable Diwali is of recent vintage. The logic behind Ma's dictum, 'Our kids don't crave for that kind of indulgence, oh no', was twofold: concealing the family's poverty and keeping kids away from crackers, which brought nothing but troubles for one and all.

Today, as we get our kids a bagful of crackers, we don't give two hoots if they will end up cracking the chimney of a lantern in a poor man's home. One such Diwali, a bomb went off in the hand of my nephew Jaimin; the impact of the blast rendered his entire hand bloodied. He was shifted forthwith to a hospital in Hatakeshwar for emergency surgical treatment. Sitting on edge throughout that night in the hospital corridor, I kept watching in a mix of surprise and horror as people burnt by crackers kept trickling in for treatment. As many as ten operations were undertaken in that private hospital that night, and yet the city, oblivious to the unfolding theatre of macabre, went gung-ho with bombs, rockets and crackers of assorted sizes and prices.

Today, our ancestral house in Rajpur still stands, surviving more as an heirloom of precious memories than anything else. Ma still lives there and still, on the night of Diwali or in the morning of the New Year, we, the sprawling family of five brothers, two sisters and their descendants, flock the place without fail. These days, just the cost of footwear we purchase for the whole family ahead of Diwali runs into half a lakh easily. In the modern-day Diwali, flooded by dry fruits, assorted sweets, fashionable apparels and filthy lucre, my time-worn eyes keep looking for a hint of the Diwali we celebrated amidst suffering, privation, hunger and penury. Though short on ostentation and prosperity, it was a Diwali no less. A Diwali high on deep delight, that.

Those Diwalis of my childhood, adolescence and youth were festivals, less of fun and frolic, and more of misery and mundanity. And yet, hardly a month after the end of the festive season, Ma would set off in her sing-song voice, speculating about the imminent arrival of the next Diwali, 'Sixteen days of Shraddh. Nine days of Navratri and the tenth is Dussehra. And then comes, close on the heels, the damsel of Diwali. Look up! It's already there, in the offing.'

7

Your Chappals, Our Skulls

Even after all this time, whenever our extended family gathers under one roof, no matter what the occasion, their conversations turn to the past, and one episode from my childhood never fails to amuse them.

The year is 1964 or 1965. I am a lisping kid of five or six. Much against his wishes, buckling under the pressure of his conservative parents, my progressive

Ba has agreed to make arrangements for the child marriages of my elder brother and sister. The wedding ceremony is to take place in Khadol, our native village in central Gujarat. Hearing that her well-to-do son, who works in a textile mill in Ahmedabad, is coming home with his family to get his children married, my grandma is elated – more elated than a Patel mother receiving her US-based son at Ahmedabad airport.

It is my first-ever train journey. Setting out early in the morning, we disembark at Anand and, from there, catch a bus to our village, arriving around noon. The preparations begin as soon as we enter the *vas*, a Chamar ghetto on Khadol's outskirts. Women pound and winnow the grain we have brought along – millet, sorghum and rice – while crooning wedding songs. Someone sets up a small, brass idol of Lord Ganesha as a part of the Ganesh Sthapana ritual. Enterprising young men go from house to house along the street, asking to borrow everyone's best sarees, and then start erecting a ceremonial tent. We children strut around in our brand-new clothes and chappals. In the rush of activities, no one notices when the night falls.

This is my first night in our native village and one which will live in my memory forever. Exhausted after a full day's work, everybody silently finds a place, here and there, inside and outside the home, to spread mattresses or just plain bedsheets on the floor and hits their makeshift beds. As night thickens outside, I doze off on a quilt in a corner, still wearing my new chappals. Assuming that I am fast asleep, Ma tries to slip them off, and I wake up with a start. When she asks that I part with my footwear, I flatly refuse. She tries to cajole me, but I am stubborn. The more she struggles to pull the chappals off, the firmer my grip on them becomes. Hearing the rising commotion, people rush over to witness the tug of war between mother and son. Quiet amusement gives way to hearty laughter, and soon the crowd is egging me on. Ba comes over too and tries to reason with me, but I remain as unyielding as a rock, inviting spanks on the back and then the butt. I cry my eyes out but emerge victorious and sleep with the spoils of war, my small feet tightly hugging those prized pair of chappals. The reason I put up such a struggle was fear – the fear of losing my brand-new chappals to a thief or a sniffing street dog. New clothes were one thing, but I really didn't want to take chances with my chappals. I had never owned a pair before. For that matter, I never used to wear any kind of footwear around our chawl, even while using the public toilets.

The 'hereditary occupation' assigned to us Chamars is tanning and cobbling. In Khadol, we shared our rear veranda with Govind, an old fart, who would sit hunched over his anvil from dawn to dusk, stitching up a great variety of footwear – chappals, *mojdi*s, cheap flat-soled slippers – as well as leather straps for waterwheels. Most other Chamar households in the vas were engaged in the same line of work. All day, the vas throbbed with the footfalls of the upper-caste Patel and Thakor women who arrived from Khadol proper to have their measurements taken. But in the casteist village economy, we Chamars were less like salespeople and more like *grahak*s, the contracted customers.[1] The residents of the Chamar vas were surprised to learn that the child of their urban caste-brother had never owned a pair of chappals before – that the son of a man who worked in a textile mill in the Manchester of India went without chappals was a bitter irony not lost on those unlettered, poor villagers. For them, it was an object lesson in how the miserable destiny of tanners persisted across geography and history.

❧

I don't remember ever wearing a pair of chappals at the municipal school in Rajpur, where I was a pupil till Class 7. Even today, when I visit my alma mater, my gaze lowers to the grimy, unshod feet of the students playing and running about. And whenever I see devotees of Lord Rama making their holy processions with the god's *paduka* down the street, bellowing their pet war cry – *Saugandh Rama ki khate hain, mandir wahin banayenge* [We swear by Rama, the temple will come up there, only there] – those children's unshod feet, walking, dangling and swinging, flash before my eyes.

In the Mahabharata, even King Dushyant was ordered to move about barefoot in Sage Kanva's ashram, as befitted the ascetic code of conduct. But at the Democratic School in Gomtipur, where the landed and genteel classes sent their scions, the capricious administration had decreed that students could not enter the premises this way. A pair of slippers in those days cost about one or one-and-a-half rupees – a paltry amount, but one that few Dalit households could afford. However, this was lost on our worthy, Savarna teachers, the Daves and Thakores who were more interested in policing divisions of caste and class than in enlightening us.

On the first day of classes, some of us barefoot students from the Dalit chawls were duly turned away at the school gate. The mix of surprise and shock I felt then remains present in my mind after all these years. As we made our unshod Hegira home, no Rama paduka came to our rescue, nor was there any kind of NGO or charity-run chappal service to help us.[2] Later in the term, if a student was caught red-handed – or rather, barefooted – they would be thoroughly thrashed by our custodians of civility.

As a good student, I managed to befriend boys from well-to-do Savarna families. Some even visited our dilapidated house in the chawl. On one such occasion, I brought down a portrait photograph of my family that hung on a flaking wall in our front room and showed it to them with great delight and pride. One of them asked, 'Why aren't you wearing chappals in the picture?' My brilliant retort: Chappals were not allowed inside the photographer's studio. Today, that framed image sits cozily on my office desk. Often, when I look at it, I marvel at the ties the artist had slipped around the necks of my brother and me. How dapper we looked, even as our unshod feet dangled from our chairs

Once upon a time, an adventurous king, forced to walk barefoot on roads that were too stony for his chariot, hit upon the idea of covering all his kingdom's streets in leather. His clever minister found him an easier and cheaper solution: Wrap your own feet in leather instead.

That is one origin story of footwear. I'm not sure when and how that modest invention turned into a status symbol in India. Even today, Dalits in several villages of South India are banned from traversing non-Dalit areas with their chappals on – the Savarna population considers it an affront. Such glaring discrimination, which persists after decades of independence, singes my soul, just as the hot asphalt roads of my childhood once burnt my tender feet.

Not that I am unfamiliar with discrimination. During childhood visits to Khadol, in the mornings, I would gape as Ma and other women from the vas, water-pots and chappals in hand, marched out in a group towards a distant scrub for a squat. They put their chappals on only after leaving the village. It wasn't until much later that I grasped the patriarchal basis of this curious behaviour. Women were considered '*paon ki juti*' – as disposable as the shoes on our feet. How dare they wear chappals in the presence of men? The same Dalit man who lorded it over his wife at home also walked through Savarna quarters with his chappals in hand – and without any dawning epiphanies.

There are so many words to describe footwear: upaan, chappals, pairs, shoes, mojdis, footwear, slippers, sandals, flat-soled slip-ons ... But this universe is reduced in the imagination of the Gujarati Dalit to just one word: *khasadan*, which (along with variations like *khasadakootun*, *khasadankhor* and *khasadanbaji*), literally means 'shoes' but connotes contempt, lowliness, uncouth behaviour, someone accustomed to beatings with shoes, and so on. How pertinent it is that Ma's eldest brother, Kalamama, peppered all his conversations with this signature line: 'Your chappals, our skulls.' Perhaps this *takiya kalam* – a mantra of life, if you will – applied to a whole generation of Dalits who grew up amid overt discrimination and unchecked feudalism. Those were the days when Dalits were beaten with khasadan at the drop of a hat. Well into the 1970s, the dominance of the Darbars in the Bhal region of Gujarat was so total that a Dalit man, seeing a pair of shoes on the threshold of his house, had to turn around and walk away. For the shoes indicated that a Darbar man was molesting his wife inside, exercising his traditional right over her body.

In 1975, when a group of young Dalit men in Golana, armed with a new consciousness of freedom and equality, challenged a Darbar, he had to jump out of the window and run for his life, leaving his shoes behind. The next day, the rapist's father stormed the vas, swore filthily at the men, women and children of about 100 Dalit families, and claimed his inviolable right to molest any untouchable woman of his choice. Though the Dalit youths were determined to put an end to institutionalized sexual exploitation, the vas elders finally made amends for their insolence by walking through the village with the rapist's torch, turban and shoes in their mouths, right up to the Darbar's house, to return his son's belongings. Perhaps that's what Kalamama meant when he said, 'Your chappals, our skulls.'

Another footwear-related memory that time has not faded. The Chamars in the vas of my mama's village never dragged carcasses; in fact, most of them didn't have anything to do with tanning. My youngest maternal uncle, Khushalmama, had made ends meet by crafting and mending shoes all his life. He procured all his trade supplies from Ahmedabad and sat outside a Bania businessman's *pedhi*, or shop, with his *peti*, his cobbler's box. In time, he came to call his peti a pedhi: Each morning, as he set out for work, he announced, for the benefit of everyone at home, that he was going to his shop. Even today, for most Chamars in the cobbling business, their peti, however modest and makeshift, is a pedhi. What a brilliant way to elevate one's low occupation! That's probably as far as *samrasata* – the Hindutvawadi's much-touted ideal of social harmony – ever really comes into being in India.

Thanks to some good teachers and the state policy of affirmative action, I finished college and secured a government job. Even then, the idea of owning leather chappals didn't tempt me. For years, I wore plastic slippers to work, until one scorching afternoon in May, when I was sipping a cup of tea in Bawari Bazar with my poet-friend Harikrishna Pathak. He systematically and sophisticatedly denounced my footwear, explaining its ill effects on his eyes. Spooked, I bought myself a pair of leather chappals from Khadi Haat on my next payday.

In time, I graduated to leather shoes and exulted for a few years in the corporate feeling they gave me. In 2001, when I was to go abroad for the first time to attend the World Conference against Racism in Durban, I purchased an expensive pair of sports shoes on the advice of better-travelled friends. My feet took a liking to them, and now I can't give the bloody things up.

These days, I spend anything between two and five thousand rupees on a pair of shoes without batting an eyelid. But that image of my young self, curled up on the floor in the Chamar vas of Khadol village, toes clinging to my very first pair of chappals, will not vanish, not even for a fleeting moment, from my old mind, which is otherwise gradually losing its grip on the past.

Critics often distinguish between the literature of sympathy and the literature of experience, posing this rhetorical question: 'Who knows the bite of the sandal better than the wearer?' Fair enough. But this is a story of a boy who seemed destined to go without chappals altogether – a boy who, for a long time, only knew footwear by its absence. Where, I wonder, are the critical theories that can appraise a story like that?

8

Rama Bhagat, an Intractable Atheist

The last time Ba spoke to me was on 13 February 1989. He wanted to clean his mouth. Three days before, he had vomited blood as the cancerous tumour in his stomach had burst open. He had been completely bedridden since then. Perhaps the tumour had metastasized, so blood kept oozing from the corners of his mouth. I had half a heart to venture out of home on the morning of the 13th; I didn't have the heart to stay back and see him suffer either. Seeing him in so much pain was gut-wrenching. So, I went to office and, around five in the evening, received the message, 'Ba is no more.'

It was about ten at night when we reached the crematorium. A dark, short, sinewy body was placed on the pyre. And within no time, the namesake of Rama, a seven-decade-old Ba, was reduced to ashes. A full stop was placed on the lifeline of a stoic yet sanguine man. What survived of him, the last remnants, were these quivering memories. A plangent serpent coiled around the hearts and minds of grieving survivors.

Once, I had asked Ba, 'From where you got the inspiration to send us kids to school, to make us educated, cultured and reasonable beings?' He had said, his old, pale eyes lost in the distance, 'We were kids then, Kuberiyo (his cousin Kuber Sava) and I. Playing and horsing around, we didn't realize when we reached in front of the *kutchehry* in the village square. Just then, the Mukhi arrived. Seeing us, he roared, "The children of bloody *dhe* … in the village square? What cheek?" and then, chased us away, landing a slap or two on our backs. I was quite young then, but the public humiliation cut deep. And I didn't go to the square ever again. But that day, I had made a resolution, "You can't stand my shadow in the square, right? One day, my children will sit right there in the kutchehry, right in your face."' And Ba redeemed his pledge by rearing us so well that we staked a claim, not just to the village kutchehry but to the state secretariat in Gandhinagar.

Forced to desert his village at an early age, Ba had migrated to Ahmedabad and started working as a labourer in a textile mill. Throughout his life, he didn't tire of comparing the awe and terror of members and leaders of Majoor Mahajan Sangh with the *dadagiri* of the present-day unions. After his first marriage failed, Ba had developed a mix of distaste and detachment for worldly, conjugal life. Then, he turned to religiosity of such crazed order that he spent every single minute of his waking hours collecting photographs and figures of assorted deities and performing ritual worship. Such was his obsession that people had begun calling him Rama *bhagat*, the devotee. However, later he did a one-eighty and became an atheist, maybe more rabid and radical than I am, and remained committed to that identity and ideology till the end of his life. In his bhagat days, he had professed his faith to a sadhu and made him his guru. The crook stayed put at Ba's house and put himself at ease as Ba played a reverent host. That apart, he laid his hand on one thing or the other in the house and rightfully took it away every time he left. One day, he took a fancy to Ba's favourite wall clock. Ba couldn't say no to the guru's demand, but the moment marked a turning point in his life. Disillusioned, he recognized the ritualistic and institutionalized religion for what it was, a clever forgery, a load of bosh. Around that time, his marriage with Ma was contracted, which proved to be the last nail in the coffin of his asceticism. He stepped into the secular life with renewed vigour and became a householder once again.

Ba's formal education had trailed up to Class 3 before he dropped out. 'The reformist, progressive and anti-caste maharaja of Baroda, Sayajirao Gaekwad, had opened school gates for the education of Dalits,' he often reminisced as he traced his educational lineage, 'but the Brahmin teachers resigned, protesting the prospect of teaching the *antyaja*, the lowest-born kids. Thus, the first generation of Dalits happened to receive education not from the Savarna or Brahmin teachers but from Muslim and Christian ones.' And yet Ba had garnered a world of knowledge over a life of curiosity, reasonable analysis and considered opinions. Nothing was out of bounds for him, be it politics, economics, society, religion, literature, culture, history, geography or astronomy. He knew enough of these areas of knowledge to participate in any discussion or debate around them and produce well-thought-out and reasoned arguments. 'Lemme explain' and 'Understood?' were his crutch phrases or catch phrases, if you will. Once, my elder sister's father-in-law, a headmaster in a village school, had come to visit us. Done with dinner, everyone sat down for a leisurely chitchat. By sheer force of habit, Ba mounted his hobby horse and galloped on with his hallmark lemme-explains and scholarly disquisitions. In those days, at every crossroads and street corner, speculations about the impending crash of the American Skylab ran rife. As the discussion veered towards the topic, Ba began to elaborate on America's geography, throwing names and coordinates like confetti. In the flow of the moment, he asked the headmaster, 'You know where America is, don't you?' And his *vevai*, the poor thing, blurted out, 'Oh yes, a stone's throw away from our Godhra …'. The man's ignorance drove Ba up the wall. 'Gentleman, how did you become a headmaster? Good heavens! Do you teach such bull to your students?' he roared. So petrified was the vevai that he wouldn't have bled if stabbed.

Those were the days of grinding poverty, as far as my family was concerned. A family of five brothers and two sisters, completely dependent on Ba's scant wages. Ma stinged on every single paisa yet struggled to make ends meet. By then, the much sought-after electricity lines had reached quite a few villages in Gujarat, but not our house in the metropolis, not before three of my kin graduated with a degree. Though ground down by acute shortages and the burden of countless social responsibilities, our parents had educated all of us. They strove to provide for our needs, legit or otherwise, by bringing suffering upon themselves, borrowing money on exorbitant interest, pawning or selling jewellery, and so on. As my elder brother cleared Senior Secondary Certificate (SSC) examination, they decided to enrol him in the agricultural university at Anand. While performing admission formalities, Ba learnt that physical training was a compulsory subject in the degree programme and the knees of the man who defied gods, society and systems turned to water. 'What if the Patel boys kicked my son in the game of kabaddi and killed him!' The fear of caste hatred prevented him from enrolling his son in the university. Later, my brother joined a science college in Ahmedabad but had to opt out of the programme in just a couple months. He then enrolled in the faculty of arts. Throughout these flip-flops and financial losses, I remember, Ba had maintained a stoical silence. Not a word of complaint or criticism. For he firmly believed that his children shouldn't feel hampered by monetary constraints when it came to choosing their career and future.

Progressive and iconoclastic thoughts ran in Ba's veins like blood. About fifty to fifty-five years ago, he had fiercely opposed the idea of performing the Hindu ritual of thirteenth-day ceremony after his father's demise. But pitted against the ultra-conservatives of those times, his opposition didn't have much purchase. The ceremony, eventually, turned out to create a mountain of debt from under which he couldn't wriggle out for his whole life; it stuck to him like a leech until he retired. My elder brother and sister, Manibhai and Kamalabehn, were forced into child marriage, much against his wishes, and those marriages collapsed like a house of cards when they reached the threshold of adulthood. Kamalabehn cleared the SSC exam and her groom failed it, which became a sore point for her in-laws, such that they began to insist, suddenly and unreasonably, on her being formally sent to her in-laws' without any further delay. Sensing the pulse in the house, Kamalabehn posed a pointed question to Ba, 'You're keen on sending me away and discontinuing my education just because I am a girl, isn't it?' The point-blank hit cut deep and the very next day, Ba initiated formalities for her divorce and admission in a college. As a result, my sister became one of the few woman graduates – so few that one could actually count them on the knuckles of one's fingers – in the whole of our *taluka*. But, when Kamalabehn's second marriage too fell apart, it proved to be a hell of a shock for Ba, with the result that his sense of outrage against the patriarchal social system became deeper and rock-hard. The failed marriages of Motabhai too gnawed at him unceasingly.

Being progressive and reform-minded, he didn't follow calcified customs and social mores as a matter of conviction. On the occasions of death or illness, he visited his relatives and acquaintances without fail to extend emotional or other support, but attending wedding ceremonies or going on post-divorce consolation visits just to backbite or bitch around never suited his righteous, fiery temperament. After retirement, he passed his days reading newspapers, magazines, books, etc., and, at times, chatting. After her second divorce, Kamalabehn got a good job, but it was far from Ahmedabad. Initially, Ma went along and stayed with her, but when that became point of dispute among my bhabhis, Ba came forward to replace Ma. Everyone wondered how a gregarious man like him, accustomed to appreciative and captive audience, would adjust to the claustrophobic environs of government quarters. But much to our surprise, Ba settled in the new place quickly and comfortably. During those last five years of his life, Kamalabehn and her darling son Atit became the veritable centre of his world.

Frankly speaking, Ma and Ba were poles apart in all respects. Ma was completely unlettered but socially prudent. Ba was a scholar but almost intransigent, just like me, when it came to belief system and values. Sometimes I wonder how on earth their conjugal life could drift on all these years without a hitch or a hurdle. Because the moments when Ba and Ma talked in concordant notes were few and far between. And yet, I have no doubt in my mind that their hearts were connected by a luminous bond of love, a unique bond that kept them from separating.

A steady, thoroughgoing bitterness remained the defining trait of Ba's personality until he breathed his last, a deep resentment against sociopolitical structures, religion and economic system. Associated with the Ambedkarite movement right from the beginning, Ba had taken memberships of the Republican Party of India (RPI) and Samata Sainik Dal (SSD). Rama Bhagat, the soldier for equality, looking dapper in blue half pants, blue shirt, blue cap and a shining pair of shoes, still leaps up from the memory of the chawl people. So total was his commitment to the ideology that even when the Majoor Mahajan Sangh enjoyed undisputed dominance over textile mills in Ahmedabad, he didn't think of becoming its member. Once, while at work, he met with a horrific accident and sustained serious injuries that confined him to bed for a long time. Even then, he chose not to seek Mahajan's help for claiming compensation from the management or any other assistance. That's Ba for you in a snapshot, the long and short of an unbending, self-respecting man.

Our house was a site of daily discussions and disputes over a great variety of questions, and Ba made it a point to participate in all of them. No amount of logic or rhetoric could get him to swallow my assessment of Babasaheb in the present context or my critique of his idea of conversion. It was anathema to him, that kind of argument – more sophistry and clever verbal gymnastics than substance. Even a tangential remark expressing disagreement with Dr Ambedkar or Ambedkarism was enough to trigger a vehement response from him. A fine testament to his single-minded devotion to Dr Ambedkar was encountered at the time of the leader's demise. How Ba wanted to pay tribute to his intellectual idol by attending his funeral procession and last rites! But because of his son's life-threatening illness, he couldn't go, something that remained a source of lifelong regret for him. Again, when the Dalits of Gujarat realized the value of Babasaheb's ideas after the anti-reservation riots of 1981, Ba's delight knew no bounds. He would read Dalit literature with great relish and often wonder aloud, 'If only such writers were around when Babasaheb was alive!' Ba was a formidable opponent of Hinduism. A staunch critic. And the one thing I am quite sure of is that no amount of reading heavy tomes and scholarly books could have afforded me the profound and prolific insights into the varna system and Hindu scriptures that Ba so casually and lucidly provided over dinner and in drawing-room discussions.

It's nothing short of a miracle that about fifty to sixty years ago, when Dalit life was weighed down by a slavish observance of tradition, superstition, holy threads and talismans and mantra-tantra, Ba could develop a scientific outlook on life in an outright rejection of ritual worship and associated hypocrisies. A bhagat once upon a time, he had turned so intractable an atheist that he never allowed even an apparently innocuous ritual of Satyanarayan Katha to take place in our house, let alone arranging a holy *havan* or other forms of Brahminical worship. Thanks to Ba's convictions, we moved into the house we live in today without what has become a must-perform rite these days: a vastu ceremony. Instead, he had organized a programme of Bhim Geet, where the famous singer of Bhim Bhajans, Shri Pagalbaba, was invited to perform. This event dates back at least forty-five years, if not more. Over years of reading and reflection, Ba had come to develop an incisive and cold-blooded critique of Hinduism and the bunch of rituals it prescribed. As far as Islam and Christianity went, he respected both, but when it came to emotional attachment, no other religion but Buddhism made the cut. He repeated it without tiring that whatever little education he could get was on account of the mission's school he had briefly attended. Whether the tattoo of the holy cross superimposed on the 'Rama' etched on the back of his right hand was his little act of conversion or just plain rebellion, I'm not sure. Perhaps it was a bit of both.

A day before his death, Ba lay in his bed, groaning and moaning in excruciating pain. When Ma told him, 'Look at the photograph of Sai Baba on the wall in front of you and recite his name. All your pain will disappear within moments.' Immediately, he turned his face away in disgust and spat out, 'What? Have you laid my bed facing your Saibabo? Change its location, right now. Do you hear?' And he couldn't rest easy until his instructions were carried out. They say that at the time of death, the *samskara* of a person's previous lives resurrect in a final bid for redemption and, thus, the man, however rabid an atheist, dies reciting the name of the Almighty. But with Rama Bhagat, it was different; he remained an estimably stable atheist through and through, as intractable in life as in death.

Regrettably, Ba's intellectual legacy was invaded and desecrated by his worldly-wise sons in his lifetime. The 'worthy' sons of a man who had not given two hoots to rituals like Griha Pravesh in times much more orthodox and vindictive, couldn't muster the courage to enter the small house they had purchased without a vastu ceremony. And all of it, the shameful show and ostentation, was performed in Ba's presence in verbatim conformity with the codes of Hindu rituals. Ironically, the thirteenth-day ceremony of a man who had been a lifelong adversary of Hinduism was performed with due religious pomp and ritualistic glitter; a Hindu bhajan singer was invited to sing bhajans for the peace and deliverance of the soul of the deceased; Ba's cremated remains were immersed in the Reva, and a Shraddh too was performed in his honour and for his blessings.

Offspring are the mirror images of their parents, so goes the popular saying. But the proverbial similarity, to my mind, should extend beyond outward appearance to intellectual apparatus, especially when the ideas of parents are fairer, more just and futuristic. None of us could gainsay the fact that we failed to follow Ba's ideas in their entirety.

In my case, Ba's inheritance has not been limited to a short stature and a dark skin tone. I have inherited the staggering height of his reformist thoughts and the dazzling brilliance of his progressive mind. Thanks to this intellectual legacy, I had refused to sit teary-eyed in snow-white apparel after his demise and be the sorry receptacle for the condolences of the visitors. I had resumed my duties at the office on the third day after he left. Neither did I attend the thirteenth-day ceremony, organized in his honour and for a peaceful afterlife of his soul, nor did I accept ceremonial offerings from his Shraddh. And, mind you, this was neither a form of escapism nor a proud exhibition of my progressivism. Just a consciously developed faith in Ba's ideals. Yes, that's what it was.

It's been six months since Ba left his mortal body and, yet, I can feel his presence in this house. Echoes of lemme-explain rock my bedroom in the middle of the night. At such moments, I wake up with a start and the agony of witnessing the helplessness and the inability of his children to internalize all that Ba so passionately upheld and stood for washes over me. The jet-black night then floods my sleepless eyes and drowns me in the pitch-dark of painful memories.

9

Sonny of a Sane Mother

At ninety plus, Ma left, having led a full, fulfilling life and leaving behind a lush green orchard of a flourishing family. Such deaths are not to be grieved but celebrated, the worldly-wise often counsel. And yet, a sea of tears burst forth on all sides when Ma breathed her last. The mood in the house was doom and gloom as four generations of the Maheria family had been orphaned in one fell swoop. All eyes dripped on unchecked, not just of her children but even of her daughters-in-law with whom Ma had a bitter-sweet relationship. My bhabhi, the widow of my eldest brother, cried her heart out the way she hadn't even over the premature demise of her husband a decade ago. The refrain of her heart-rending keening was, 'Ma was Ma, nobody can ever replace her.' Dakshabhabhi, who had a tough time with Ma in the initial years after her marriage, too wept inconsolably. To everyone who tried to console her, she said, 'Married off at a tender age, I could spend only the first fifteen years with my real mother. But Ma had been a mother to me for twenty-five years.' My eyes had begun to ooze from the day Ma had caught the corona bug, but the tears that had streamed down discreetly until now suddenly burst forth, like a failed dam, and carried me away. Never in my life have I cried so much nor will I, I'm sure, cry so bitterly ever again.

Ma was hospitalized in February 2020 while she was staying with my younger brother Raju. And then, the pandemic and the sudden national lockdown changed everything. In those difficult times, all of us had been extra careful to shield her from an infection. For the last several years, Ma had been hung up, quite curiously, on medicines and dispensaries, and wouldn't listen to reason. An unhealthy obsession with health. But this time round, she listened to our counsel and didn't venture out. Perhaps she had caught on to the lethality of the virus. On our part, we too ensured that she remained indoors, except for the trip she undertook from Raju's place to Dinesh's, my other brother. In her dotage, winters went especially hard on her, though her body was relatively free from any major diseases or serious ailments, except those related to ageing. By December that year, however, it got into her to return to Gandhinagar and see her family doctor. Ma's word was an inviolable decree to us. The day she came here, she changed her mind and insisted on being taken to Dr Ashwin Gadhavi's hospital in Gomtipur. I tried to reason with her as to how risky it was, coaxed and cajoled her, but to no avail. A couple of visits to the hospitals in Ahmedabad did the trick, and Ma got infected with the virus.

Willy-nilly, we admitted her to the Covid hospital in Ahmedabad as there was no other option in sight. I reached out to all those contacts and connections who could be of help to ensure that Ma got the best of the treatment and care. The sons of my elder brother kept visiting the hospital on a daily basis without fearing for their life and catered to each of her needs. We couldn't have endured those twenty-two days of utmost trepidation but for the doctor's assurances, the video calls of my kin with Ma and the bulletins from sources about her improving health. Ma had not been put on a ventilator even once and she was doing fine on room air, something that gave strength to our hope that she'd soon be discharged.

On 26 January 2021 I did the unthinkable, attended a video call from Ma, something I had avoided doing out of the fear that I wouldn't be able to handle it. No one else was present in the house. She would be discharged the next morning, she said, and then, in an unexpected gesture, joined her hands. I too responded with a namaste, completely innocent of the fact that this was to be the last of my interactions with her, that she had bid me a final goodbye. That evening, I had personally spoken to the doctor on duty in Ma's ward and confirmed that she was stable. But destiny had different plans ... Around midnight, I received the news of Ma's demise. It was a shocker for us, a bolt from the blue. Ma, who was to return home the next morning, had left forever, leaving her kids in the lurch.

The morning of 27 January brought me face to face with the lifeless body of Ma, zipped in a PPE kit, the dead body of a woman whom I had never seen at ease or folding her legs in her long, luminous life. Having completed her final rites and the telephonic condolence meeting, I was in two minds about attending the ceremony of immersing Ma's *asthi*, the post-cremation physical remains, in the Reva near Chandod. But I broke the vow I had observed through the life and undertook that difficult journey, the journey of carrying in my lap the last remains of Ma, in whose lap we had sought refuge through the thick and thin of life. That scorching afternoon on the riverbank in a way became a metaphor for Ma's life, spent in constant, unending struggles. The moments in which the asthis were poured into a copper plate for the performance of rites turned heavy, almost frozen in time. About an hour later, an asthi-filled earthen pot was set afloat in the flowing waters of the Reva amidst tears streaming down our cheeks. As the last vestige of her mortal body dissolved, we were left bereft, clinging hopelessly to memories that were to haunt us for life.

Ma came from a very affluent family, I'm told. Her father and grandpa had thrown a grand community feast to celebrate her birth and sent the guests off with a rupee coin bearing the Queen's image – a substantial sum in those days. But she was a victim of child marriage, an evil deeply entrenched in caste groups lower down in the varna hierarchy. At a tender age, maybe in the year of India's independence, she became a mother and the very next year, a widow. Hapless and hopeless, she returned to her parents, only to find that they considered their young, widowed daughter a burden and a social stigma, and hoped to contract her remarriage. Their search for a suitable match ended with Ba. Leaving her son in the care of his childless uncle, Ma came far away from her village to set up the household of a darkie widower with a daughter. Learning about what they thought was a case of glaring mismatch, the neighbours and acquaintances had denounced Ma's brothers: 'Fie on you! You've thrown the poor girl into a ditch.' But Ma, it seemed, had accepted it, the life in a dark, smelly ditch, not out of resignation but a resolve to sacrifice her being in the baking, blazing furnace of suffering and emerge victorious, shining like gold.

An earnest but callow village lass, Ma came to Ahmedabad and began to bring Ba, who had become a bhagat after a failed marriage, back to the rigours and joys of secular life bit by bit. Without crossing swords or locking horns with anyone, she deftly wriggled her own unique way out of the expectations, legit or otherwise, of her stepdaughter, of the vast family of her in-laws and her own maternal family, which was equally large and demanding. 'Thrift is the income of the third brother,' she often quoted the popular proverb, 'and that is the woman of the house. Managing household affairs is her lookout. Your Ba earned all of thirty rupees a month. The poor thing didn't know how I made ends meet, just as you don't have the foggiest idea of how we reared and educated you, caught in the whirlpool of social responsibilities.' I have seen the jaws of people drop as they spoke of Ma's life struggle as first-hand witnesses, their praise total and unqualified: 'If this Dahi wasn't around, Rama's house would have gone to dogs.' Indeed, providing for our sprawling family was Ma's exclusive lookout. For Ba was a bhagat, both literally and figuratively. An ascetic in all mundane matters. Had Ma not functioned as a central, unifying force in the family and mediated its relationship with the community and society at large, none of us would have reached where we are today.

Ma undertook back-breaking work in factories as a daily-wager and went to textile mills on holidays as a contractual housekeeping staff. Quickly finishing the household chores, she would step out to undertake long, tiring expeditions to collect cow dung, logs of wood, tinder and sawdust. Stand for hours together in the Fair Price shop for food rations and rush us to dispensaries and hospitals when we fell ill. As if this daily hustle and bustle weren't enough of a drain on her energy, she had to worry over accurate and advance planning for things like light, water and toilets, the basic civic facilities we could have in our house only in dreams. Amidst all these headaches, my unlettered Ma, who couldn't make out whether the book in her hands was held the right way or upside down, kept a keen, vigilant eye on our education. Not only did she send us to school without fail but she also ensured that we didn't skip homework and learnt mathematical tables and the alphabet by heart. As we sat around her, the paraphernalia of our textbooks and notebooks spread out for her to inspect, she looked to us a real, stern headmistress. Not just us, she had brought up the sons of her two widower brothers like her own as well, and when they fell out with her after their marriage, her motherly heart was deeply lacerated. But the self-respecting woman who knew how to take the pain and anguish in her stride snapped all bonds with them with the same dagger that had lodged in her heart and didn't give them so much as a second look for the rest of her life.

My birth had kicked off a cyclone of troubles in Ma's life. The postpartum condition she had developed drained her of all vitality. That debilitation continued even after I grew up, now morphed into a deep anguish over my problematic attitudes and rash, radical behaviour. My intellectualism made her decidedly uneasy, but her refrain, 'Let him do what he thinks fit' always helped her reconcile with my position. She had welcomed my decision to remain unmarried, for example, but the resolution of not attending weddings of anybody, even if it was my blood brother, was simply beyond her; it disturbed her no end. At the time of the wedding of my elder brother, I was in Class 9. Since I didn't want to attend the ceremony, I left home early in the morning without telling anyone where I was going and without caring for the tearing anxiety this would cause Ma. Around midnight, when I returned, I had expected a scene, but Ma did not utter anything harsh or cross. Just said, 'Ultimately, you had it your way, right?' and that's that. After I got a government job, I left home in a huff over some issue and sojourned at my half-brother Kantibhai's in Amraiwadi, Ahmedabad. Every day, he dropped and picked me up on his Luna bike at a point near Sukhramnagar from where I took the staff bus. Ma was privy to this *tamasha*, which had been going on for a few days. One day, she came over and hid behind a shop near Sukhramnagar. As soon as I got down from the bus, she came up to me, outrage burning in one eye and compassion in the other. Then, we began to walk without a word and kept plodding for fifteen minutes in heavy but meaningful silence. Back at home, too, neither she nor anyone else behaved as if anything was amiss. Abnormal, crazed behaviour has been more of a norm with me, but Ma, whose happiness or otherwise lay in the joys and sorrows of her children, never so much as taunted me about it, not once in all these years.

She was extremely fearless, and more than once in all these years I had been a marvelling witness to her matchless courage. In 1969, the year of Gandhi's birth centenary, horrific communal riots had caught the city in their crushing grip. Taking advantage of a brief relief in the curfew clampdown, Ma had set out without a second thought, plodding along desolate railway tracks on her own and with small kids in tow, from Rajpur to Maninagar, from where she wanted to take a train to Nadiad and leave us kids in the custody and safety of her parental home. I was ten years old then. Thereafter, Ahmedabad kept turning into a flashpoint of caste and communal riots, and we kept witnessing Ma's exceptional daring with a mix of awe and horror. When Mahijikaka, Ba's brother, was down with tuberculosis and his wife had walked out on him in a huff, Ma moved to our native village Khodal in Anand district and nursed him for days on end. Hardly familiar with the coordinates of Baroda, she single-handedly took Kaka, as his condition worsened, to a hospital in the city for treatment. When my younger brother Dinesh got a job at Rajkot, it was Ma who travelled all the way to set up his house there. Not once did the all-too-normal anxiety about being unlettered and getting lost on the way cross her mind when it came to intercity or intra-metropolis travel.

Ma had seen death at close quarters. Her parents and in-laws had passed away when she was quite young. That apart, she had been a tragic witness to about three dozen deaths in the families on both sides: brothers and sisters-in-law, sister and brothers-in-law, nephews, and so on. After Ba's demise, Ma lived on for about three decades. Two of her sons and a stepdaughter had breathed their last with Ma by their side. When Motabhai passed away suddenly, and shockingly for all of us, at the age of fifty-seven, I had thought that Ma wouldn't be able to get over it and wouldn't live long. But she soldiered on for another decade, as if to provide emotional support to her widowed daughter-in-law and restore the family to a sense of stability and normalcy. Ultimately, she left the world with Motabhai's residential address on her death certificate.

But I have seen the same Ma, courageous and unyielding as she was, giving in to dank hopelessness and depression. When the failure of as many as three marriages of my elder brother were attributed to her being a difficult mother-in-law, Ma slipped into dark despair. If there was one aspect of her character that I loved the most, it was her partiality for her daughters. I don't think she ever loved her sons more than her daughters, nah. If it came to choosing whose suffering she would partake of, Ma would side with her daughters without so much as a second thought, I'm sure. She was an exception to the rule in this regard, a rarity among mothers. After her matriculation exams, when Kamalabehn, my elder sister, was hospitalized, Ma had stayed with her for days on end without caring for her own health or well-being. It was she who had propped up a glum and gloomy Ba when he had virtually collapsed after filing a divorce application for his daughter. When Kamalabehn's second marriage fell apart, she looked up to no one else but Ma for succour, which she provided with absolute emotional commitment until the former became a graduate, got a government job and attained financial self-sufficiency. When she got her first posting in a back-of-beyond region in Sabarkantha, it didn't take Ma a moment to chuck all her responsibilities towards her husband, sons and daughters-in-law and make a beeline for that deserted, faraway location. Her love for my youngest sister Anju was ineffably profound and endless. Anju too paid it back, the heaving sea of affection Ma showered on her, by looking after her with matchless devotion all her life. Atit and Anagat, sons of Kamalabehn and Anju, respectively, were apples of Ma's eyes; not just us, but the whole world paled into insignificance before them.

Ma often fondly reminisced about the jewellery she had brought along in her trousseau: large circular earrings, low-hanging multi-bell earrings, pipe-thick necklace, heavy battened bracelets and anklets weighing 750 grams. Selling and mortgaging this silver and gold jewellery as and when required, borrowing money at exorbitant interest and drudging away the better and greater part of her life, Ma had educated us in a way we never felt deprived. And yet she never said anything that even tangentially conveyed her bitterness or her deep-seated longing for her lost ornaments. Not even something as innocuous as, 'My unslaked desires will come to haunt you when I am gone.' Rather, her pet refrain was, 'What is all this to me? All I want is the good of the family ... Whatever little I've got in return is good enough for me ... As if I am going to live forever to retain a stake over it.'

Even after all of us settled down to a good life, Ma neither heaved a sigh of relief nor put herself at ease. For after Ba's departure, she felt that her responsibilities had increased a thousand-fold. My elder brother Mehulbhai's children, whose wisdom and education didn't seem to grow with age, were a source of her constant worries. 'I bitched about out-of-line children of others, and that's why perhaps God has condemned me with similar children.' The surging pain of her heart often tumbled out in such self-blaming outbursts. Perhaps she had chosen an educated bride for Dinesh because she felt that she had burnt her fingers with the other daughters-in-law who were uneducated and, on that account, unwise.

Ma's attachment to the Rajpur house, where her joint family lived and thrived, bordered on obsession. She saw herself as a weaver bird that had built that nest bit by bit and straw by straw. It was her principality, that modest house, and she, a power centre, a powerhouse.

She always insisted that all of us, the brothers and their families, stayed there, the space crunch, unfulfilled modern needs and struggles of commuting to our workplace notwithstanding. Of course, when her sons erected or purchased better accommodations elsewhere, her joy knew no bounds, but the idea of making those posh structures home didn't go down well with her. She herself had bought a small house, a one-room-kitchen variety, in Maninagar, ironically from Ba's *maranmudi* – the money set aside for one's funeral rites – while he was alive. But that house had ended up becoming our refuge during riots and curfew only; none of us ever made it our permanent abode.

After her initial protestations, all of us brothers eventually left Rajpur and went our separate ways, but Ma stayed back. Despite our insistence and pleadings, she didn't accompany any of us to our new homes. Even when her youngest son left her nest, Ma stayed put, like a rock. Arrangements for her tiffin were made. In 2013, when Kamalabehn retired, Ma buckled under pressure from me and agreed to join us in Gandhinagar. That I had taken her, by pure coincidence, to Rajpur just before she caught the corona bug is the only consolation, nay a huge relief, we have now.

The presiding deity in Ma's religious heart was Lord Satyanarayana. She began her day by chanting victory to the god, the only source of hope in her life. A woman as generous as she was truthful and optimistic, Ma never tired of running around for the welfare of her family, neighbours, remote acquaintances, even random passers-by and, thus, won glad, grateful hearts, almost in hundreds. Thus, my Dahima, literally a sane mother, was Ma to many. 'Is there anything we humans can stake a claim on when we pop off?' was her pet rhetorical question and refrain when someone asked her to just slow down and look after herself. The latest fad amongst the progressives and karmashila from Maharashtra, which has been nationalized to a certain extent now, is to use mother's instead of father's name as one's middle name, but thanks to Ma and her widespread fame, we, Dahima's children, haven't felt the need to do so. For when Motabhai worked as a ticket checker on Ahmedabad railway station, the acquaintances who ran into him on platform, addressed him not as Maheria Saheb or such like but simply as Dahima's son. Up until the old guard of Rajpur–Gomtipur was in flesh and blood, I too answered to the call of *Dahimano dikaro*, sonny of the sane mother, whenever I visited Rajpur. Ma often used this lovely moniker, actually a popular idiom in Gujarati, to designate well-educated, well-bred and wise lads of Bania-Brahmin families and asked us to be one. Today, armed with education and plum jobs, we have lived up to her dream and become Dahima's sons, both literally and figuratively. And Dahima has played no small part in the accomplishment of that feat.

It's the destiny and the bounden duty of an offspring to light the pyre of the one who birthed them. But can I ever say that Ma brought me in this world and I repaid the debt by performing the ritual of cremation? Does the matter really end there? Abu Kasai's chawl throbbed with as many as fifty Dalit households and the much-maligned benefit of reservation in government jobs was available to them as well. However, hardly five households could benefit from the provision because the rest couldn't fulfil the basic precondition for availing reservation, i.e., education. That we could escape the hellish life in Rajpur redounds less to our natural genius and much more to the education our parents gave us by undertaking gruelling labour themselves and never harnessing us kids to it, no matter how abject our poverty and how crippling the privations. That we could graduate from living in a squat house with tin-sheet roof to double-floored pucca tenements. That those who dithered perennially over purchasing a bicycle could become proud owners of four-wheelers (all my siblings except me). That those accustomed to seeing their parents selling and pawning ornaments and beg-borrow money all around could invest in fixed deposits and mutual funds. Those who grew up in a house without windows, let alone a fan, could inhabit air-conditioned homes and offices. That we could organize pilgrimages, not just to local places like Zanzarka, Ranunja or Chotila but as far as Tirupati, for Ma who couldn't spare so much as twenty-five paisa to undertake a trip to Pavagadh when we were young.

Leave aside these material comforts and affluence for a second; one can always do without them. But that we could grow up to be model civilians, free from addiction, ignorance and violence, while living in an area where gambling, filthy abuses and fisticuffs were the order of the day. The credit for all of it goes to the education and the training none but Ma gave us.

For about five months before she passed away, Ma was staying with my youngest brother Dinesh. On 5 September 2020, celebrated as Teachers' Day in India, his wife shared a pic of Ma reading the newspaper in the family's WhatsApp group with a caption that read, 'Though unlettered, Ma can't do without newspaper every morning. Kudos to the illiterate woman who educated all of us. Let's bow our heads before a real teacher on Teachers' Day.' Reading that homage, which beautifully echoed the feelings of the entire family, to Ma's work of a lifetime from her 'educated daughter-in-law', my whole being had become awash with a sense of deep, quiet satisfaction. The famous Marathi Dalit writer Daya Pawar dedicated his autobiography to his mother with these words: 'Ma, I could feel the colossal pain of the Dalits just because of you.' If I happened to write such a book in the future, its dedication would be, 'Ma, I could feel all the happiness of the world just because of you.'

10

Those Years in Dhoraji

I was just about two years away from retirement when I got a promotion and, along with it, marching orders for a place 350 kilometres away from Gandhinagar: Shree Bhagvatsinhji High School in Dhoraji, a taluka headquarters in Rajkot district. Going that far was not advisable, said most of my relatives and well-wishers. But the prospect of having a new, different experience set me on the road to Dhoraji on 15 June 2015.

Three centuries ago, there was nothing but dense, daunting forest in the place we now know as Dhoraji. That's perhaps why Chunilal Madia, the eminent Gujarati novelist and a native of Dhoraji, called it a township born of a mote-hill. And rightly so! For as one moved from Tran Darwaja to Darbargarh, one would realize that the town's terrain was like a camel's hump. Over the years, it became populated, first by the Charans who set up their *nesa*, a cluster of shepherds' huts and cowsheds, on the hill. The income from agricultural produce and milk products drove them to settle down and convert the nesa into a small hamlet. The hamlet was led by a woman called Dhori Aai, a brave woman with exceptional leadership skills after whom the place got christened as Dhoraji.

Historically, Dhoraji was first captured by the Sumaras, a band of thieves, hunters and dacoits. Their leader, Hothi Sumaro, ruled the town. Lore has it that the river on the outskirts of Dhoraji was named Safoora, after Hothi's daughter. In 1748, Dhoraji came under the rule of the Gondal monarchy. The back story is, the town was gifted to the Darbar of Gondal by the nawab of Junagadh in return for the former's help in defeating Vasant Rai Purbio, the administrator of Dhoraji. Eventually, the Memons arrived and settled in Dhoraji.

In view of the town's security, the king of Gondal began to erect a fort in 1805, the last few relics of which still survive today. The fort had four main gates and three *bari*s, smaller entrances. The first settlers to arrive in Dhoraji after the inauguration of the fort were the Kanabi farmers. For Sangramji, the then king of Gondal, married to a woman from Vaghasi, a village in what is known as Anand district today, thought it expedient to get farmers from his wife's village to relocate in Dhoraji. The Kanabis, thus, are called the first settlers of Dhoraji, and to preserve their original identity, many of them have changed their surnames to Vaghasiya.

Dhoraji developed with the passage of time in line with the codes of the caste system. The place is home to people of all religions, except Christians, and all castes. Muslims account for half of the population, but the strength of the Dalits too is substantial. In days of yore, the Rajputs were settled near the fort so that they could perform their varna role, i.e., protecting the Raj, with ease and efficiency. The Dalits, the labouring classes and Muslims were settled in the southeast. The Kanabis were granted land for agriculture and residence in the middle of the state while the Brahmins were settled close to temples and the Raj.

Built in the latter half of the century and resplendent with a stately, ornate entrance, Darbargarh was a palace rich in sculptural and architectural beauty. But that archaeologically 'protected' site is in ruins now. It was here that Bhagvatsinh, the progressive and popular king, was born. Adjacent to the palace is Bhimjini Bari, a small gate leading to Baharpura, an area populated by Dalits and Muslims. The bari, in popular parlance, is called a 'putrid portal' because it has become a popular pee station. It is a living example of how careless we as people are when it comes to the preservation of our heritage, and how hollow the government claims about India being an open-defecation-free country are.

The history of the founding of Baharpura, which accommodates a fifth of Dhoraji's population, can also excite grief and outrage at the same time. Initially, the Dalits, backward castes and artisans were settled inside the fort walls, but with the advent of development, they were thrown out, evicted, asked to go *bahar*. Thus, the development and marginalization of the disadvantaged is not a story of twenty-first century exclusively, nor does Narendra Modi have any monopoly on this deadly combination. The same Baharpura was to become my address during my years in Dhoraji.

In 1881, a railway line was inaugurated between Dhola and Dhoraji. In view of the development that railway connectivity was to spark off, the map of the place was redrawn and, accordingly, the underprivileged living within the fort walls were evicted. Thus, Baharpura of today is still bahar – *outside* the town and, with no proper roads, gutter lines, banks or schools, *outside* the imagination of developers and policymakers. The proverbial *vikas* doesn't touch it even tangentially; perhaps it has been asked by executive decree of a democratic state not to stray too far. The first Dalit mayor of Dhoraji stays there and so do the Muslim representatives. In our representative democracy, Baharpura has a stake and representation but not in the roots, let alone fruits, of development. What is amusing is that Baharpura is home to world-famous *dargah*s of revered Sufi saints Khwaja Mohkam Din Serani and Lalasha Bapu. In the month of Aso every year, an 'Urs Mubarik', a death anniversary commemoration for the saint, is held here. Attended by thousands of people from far and beyond, the Urs holds pride of place among the great and grand fairs held across Saurashtra. And for the four days of Urs, Baharpura, its squalor and state of utter neglect still in place, shines with dazzling lights and the zeal and faith of tourists and devotees.

My workplace in Dhoraji was going to be a school named after Maharaja Bhagvatsinh, the school where Chunilal Madia had studied between 2 July 1932, and 31 March 1939. A matter of surging delight and great thrill, which unfortunately ebbed away on 16 June 2015, when, on my first visit, the school welcomed me with four cannons, painted in the three colours of the Indian flag, stationed at four corners of a huge quadrangle beyond the entrance. The symbolism of a cannon at the gate of a school, instead of a pen or a book, was deeply shocking. I didn't realize then that I would be in for more shocks in the next two years.

The foundation stone of the school was laid by Bhagvatsinh on 1 January 1926. The school operated from two locations: the old school building in Galaxy Chowk and the new one on the railway station road. A bustling hub of education once, the school was a picture of desolation. Apparently, not enough students took admission there. Thus, out of forty-five classrooms, only four were in use for students of Classes 9 to 12. A helipad had been installed on campus, and the quadrangle sported a barren look. After a few months, I espied small mounds of clay at five to ten locations in the quadrangle. Must be the mini mounts erected by children to worship Mohalla Mata, the holy Mother of the Street, my city-bred mind assumed. But my cute illusion was shattered when my colleagues said that they were snake hills.

During the two-year sojourn, my encounters with different people proved to me again and again the greater glory of Shree Bhagvatsinhji High School and its excellent education. A big businessman from Mumbai drove in with family in his expensive car one afternoon and spoke to me, appreciatively and at length, of the school's formative and foundational role in his success. His eyes moistened and voice choked as he remembered his teachers and classmates. I would never forget the way he circumambulated the school's building, his feet unshod and head bowed, five times before leaving. About four-and-a-half decades ago, when the state decided to close the old school and convert the building into government offices, the whole town had taken to the streets and organized protests under the banner of High School Saving Committee. A young man from the Patidar community named Ashwinkumar Chunilal Mavani was martyred in the agitation on 8 January 1981. A cenotaph commemorating him still stands in Dhoraji as a testament to people's preference for government education and the heroic struggle they waged for it. It's a different matter that, pitted as it was against the insolent might of the state, the protest didn't last long, and the government eventually slaughtered the state-funded school at the altar of privatization and the logic of market. Thus, the old school was shuttered in 2011, and the office of subdivisional magistrate took over the space. And plans are already afoot for erecting a huge multistorey building there with a capacity for accommodating all government offices in Dhoraji. It is just a matter of time before Madia's school is razed to the ground.[1] But perhaps I am exaggerating. When the Alfred High School in Rajkot, where Gandhiji studied, can be converted into a museum, what chance does Madia's school stand? If the old Bhagvatsinh high school is dead, the new one is on its deathbed.

❧

The first school came up in Dhoraji in 1906, and it was as early as 1934 that the State of Gondal issued a decree for compulsory and free primary education. About a decade and a half before introducing this progressive policy, the state had made primary education mandatory for girls. The first school for girls, founded in 1887, still stands tall in the town as a symbol of the state's commitment to women's education. A private school called Volunteers' Union Highschool was founded in 1915 by an organization committed to education and, interestingly, the funds for its maintenance were raised by holding a lottery.

In the era of privatization of education, Dhoraji has fallen for the glamour and glitz of self-financed schools, leaving the grant-in-aid schools sulking and on the back foot. The state's convoluted logic in letting the private institutions mushroom stands on the lame excuse of curtailing the flourishing industry of private tuition classes.

The names of the schools in Dhoraji curiously foreground a different and diverse history of the place. The town has a Muslim school – yes, you read it right – and a school called Patel Vidyamandir. If there are modern schools with English names like Best, Unique and Royal, there are also ones with ancient names like Chanakya, Gopal, Nachiketa, Arjun and Sandipani. That apart, Dhoraji boasts two colleges that offer undergraduate programmes in arts, commerce and management, a technical high school and a madrasa. But the two government schools in a place touted as the Hub of Education are struggling to survive despite competent teachers and committed principals.

❧

During my brief stay, whenever I saw Patidar students from surrounding villages and towns flock to Dhoraji, aboard expensive luxury buses, to take board examinations, my mind raced down the memory lane to the year 1979 when I had to walk 5 kilometres to reach the examination centre for my Class 12 exams. Surprisingly, the condition of Dalit students, taking their exams in Dhoraji, was no better than mine three and a half decades ago. However, the history of Dalit education in Dhoraji is not as cruel. Thanks to the sustained efforts of two non-Dalit advocates, Motichand Vrajlal Parekh and Mohanlal Nagji Chinai, two schools for Dalit children were founded in the year the Poona Pact was signed. I wonder how many of Dalit youth today would know this history. The Harijan Sevak Sangh had opened a hostel exclusively for Dalit students, called Thakkarbapa Chhatralaya, on Junagadh Road in 1955. Not getting any financial assistance from the state for many years now, the hostel has survived on the support of local government servants. Today, several posh caste hostels, mostly for Patidar students, have come up in Dhoraji, which is the case elsewhere too. But the non-Dalit communities in Dhoraji and even the Harijan Sevak Sangh are indifferent and impervious to the proper functioning of the Chhatralaya. So much for the equality of education and samrasata after so many years of independence!

The cankers of feudalism and casteism in Saurashtra are still intact. Alive and kicking, in fact. Being aware of that reality, I was primed for all kinds of troubles and challenges I was to encounter in the peninsula. One thing I was not to worry my head over was the hassle of house-hunting as I was going to get a government quarter. The caste-curious question, *Tame Keva?*, is quite casually thrown at anyone and everyone in Saurashtra, regardless of their being native or outsider, young or old, and so on. Encountering it in the fifty-seventh year of my life, after not having been asked to answer it in the first fifty-six years, was a hell of a shock for me. But during those years in Dhoraji, I must have answered it at least fifty-six times. On the very first day, a Muslim rickshaw driver asked me, 'What (caste) are you?' and a non-Dalit colleague in my office, not content with my answer to *Tame Keva?*, burrowed deeper with finer queries in an attempt to ferret out my sub-caste as well. If you said, you're a Dalit, your interlocuter would sport an oddly quizzical, slightly irritated look. An SC, on the other hand, would elicit feigned ignorance. The sly noser wouldn't rest easy until you gave him what he wanted, i.e., Harijan. However, I must confess that none of the people who knew about my being a 'Harijan' has ever practised untouchability with me. Every day, I took lunch with my non-Dalit colleagues as their equal and the Brahmins of Pandya Lodge, where I had dinner, never made me conscious of my caste identity. But I must underline the fact that the attitude of the upper castes wasn't above board all the time. For I didn't even realize when and how my initial residential address in Jamanavad, a non-Dalit area, got changed to Baharpura. My colleagues from Baharpura didn't recall a time when their non-Dalit coworkers visited them to ask after their health or on occasions of joy or grief in their families. In weddings and other social ceremonies, non-Dalit staff invite their Dalit colleagues for sure, but they won't attend similar events their Dalit colleagues organized, oh no. In reparation for the discrimination, they would send over *chandalo*, a sum of money as a token of love and wishes, and throw a party in the office the next day, ordering food from outside. Once, my office staff attended the wedding of an OBC peon's son with their families in tow, but none showed up at the wedding ceremony of a Dalit peon's daughter the very next week. When asked, they said the food in case of the former is generally proper, slightly purer.

Watching for the first time a dignified, peaceful procession of the dead, accompanied by mellifluous bhajans and melodious crooning, gently streaming down the road, I was greatly impressed. And learning about a common crematorium in the town for the entire Hindu community was a pleasant surprise. (The real reason behind it, I later figured out, was shortage of land.) But not even once in my stint did I see such a procession taken out for a Dalit body, or a Hindu Dalit being cremated with due ritual performance. Assuming that the Dalits bury their dead, a separate space was earmarked for them. Thus, though the crematorium was common, it was partitioned along the logic of caste.

Similarly, the busts of various leaders, installed in the town for over a century, gave me a sense of how diverse communities inhabiting a common space traced tenuous borders of caste around them, which sealed them off in thought and action. In 1934, a bust of Maharaja Bhagvatsinh was installed near the railway station. After Independence, the Dhoraji municipality placed a bust of Gandhiji near Tran Darwaja. On 22 April 1989, the Meghval Seva Samaj unveiled the bust of Dr Babasaheb Ambedkar in Galaxy Chowk in the presence of Maisaheb Dr Savita Ambedkar. Finally, a bust of Sardar Patel came up near the toll booth in 1993. Sadly, the Dhoraji of Bhagvatsinh and Gandhiji was eventually divided into one of Ambedkar and the Sardar by people who knew the life and work of none of those greats. Thank God, it hasn't yet got into the head of some crank Dhorajian, following the lead of Sadhu Satchidanand, to rechristen the town named after Dhori Aai as Bhagvatnagar to mark it as the birthplace of the maharaja.

Dhoraji is just about 25 kilometres from Junagadh and a hundred from Rajkot, Jamnagar and Porbandar.

When I reached, it was in the throes of getting an underground drainage system. Broken roads and a reign of dust defined it. The maharaja had erected a community hall – Madia's collection of plays *Rangada* was dedicated to it – for the entertainment of farmers, but present-day Dhoraji was the poorer for it. Thus, the only places I could go to, when loneliness and tedium got the better of me, were the Parag Library of the Brahma Samaj, the railway platform and the newly constructed Swaminarayan temple.

A word about the social life of the town. Jetpur road got up and going at dawn and quietened down at eventide, unlike Baharpura that stayed stark awake 24/7. The main bazar habitually kept snoring until late in the morning. Jamanavad was no more a monopoly of any one caste. The erstwhile market of sugarcane and cotton was now reborn as plastic bazar. A large part of trade and commerce had slipped from the hands of the Memons and was owned by the Patels. Dalits and Muslims earned their living by working in the construction industry. The town, though not untouched by material prosperity, was yet to modernize.

Like Dhori Aai and Safoora, Nand Kunwarba, the progressive royal lady who had said no to purdah, had bestowed a proud identity on Dhoraji. Unfortunately, she too had been reduced to a titular presence in the women's charitable hospital named after her. For I never came across a young couple chatting or laughing together in public, nor did I see the students at Girls' School step out of the premises during the recess. Even the few girls, who moved about in modern attire, looked scared and scarred. The whole social climate was stifled by an orthodox restrictive 'modesty' that locked men and women in gender roles and sexualized their bodies.

In addition to this general thrum of life, what I happened to observe at close quarters was Muslim life, their social mores, festivals, and so on. Dhoraji's Muslim population was concentrated in the area between Tran Darwaja and Langhamatam, where I went every morning for breakfast and a copy of the newspaper. The blackboards outside the mosques in the area announced the demise of someone or the other in Arabic written in Gujarati script. I found it odd that the next generation of the community couldn't read or write Arabic and yet, its obsession with Arabic identity was as crazed and constant as ever. About half of Dhoraji's population was Muslim. More than forty mosques relayed *azan* over loudspeakers. During Ramzan, sirens rang out from time to time, announcing the beginning and the ending of the roza. To be frank, nowhere else had I seen the breathtaking variety of sweets and meat as I did in Dhoraji. I had heard of the customs of mass weddings and mass *upanayan* ceremony, prevalent among the Hindus, but when I learnt from the newspaper about a mass circumcision camp for 251 children that was successfully organized in Dhoraji, I was struck dumb with horror. Had Dhoraji conveniently forgotten the rich intellectual legacy of Bhagvatsinh and Nand Kunwarba? How many of those Muslims knew that Yunus Chitalwala, the author of *Vijali Haji Kasimni*, the young researcher-critic Farooq Shah and their brilliant and progressive community brethren stayed in their midst in Dhoraji?

A town with marked differences and breathtaking peculiarities, this. For someone who was familiar with just one surname, Patel, for the Patidars based in Ahmedabad and Gandhinagar, the sheer diversity of them I encountered in Dhoraji was just mind-boggling: Makati, Jivani, Mavani, Chaniyara, Babariya, Mankadiya, Dalsaniya, Jagani, Savaliya, Sanghani, Gajera, Unghad, Vasoya, Vachhani, Kalariya, Ramoliya, Jarsaniya, Hirpara, Vekariya, Radadiya, Pansuriya, Bhimani, Thummar, Thesiya, Kaneriya, Kanasagra, Kakadiya, Tilala, Baldha, Mathukiya, Gadhethariya, Chavadiya, Patoliya, Usadaliya, Polara, Panbhar, Bodar, Sudani, Trada and Boghra. Even among Dalit surnames, I had known only Parmar, Solanki, Chavda and Rathod, but Dhoraji had a rich diversity of them: Bhasa, Bhaskar, Choravada, Singal, Khimsuriya, Vanol, Musadiya, Aghera, Vaghera, Padaya, Miyatra, Vadiyatar, Maghara, Varsur, Bavarfad, Varagiya and Bharadiya.

If there was a Bavla Chowk in the town, there was also an Aveda Chowk and a Chamadiya Kuva Chowk, a Swati Chowk, and so on. Vaghasiya Square was counterbalanced by Baldha Square, just as the main bazar was by the river bazar and flea market , held every Sunday. The town had a Kareena–Karishma nightwear and undergarment shops and a Hollywood Ladies' Tailor shop. Dhoraji accommodated posh hospitals and specialist doctors alongside bonesetters and quacks. A staggering fifty mobile phone shops and half that number of medical stores. Here, one got a 'cutting', half a cup of tea, at five bucks but the minimum auto fare was twenty rupees. A packet of Amul Milk was sold two rupees above the maximum retail price. The hair-cutting salon in Baharpura offered a paid service of *hamam*, a bathroom for a post-haircut shower. There were no bookshops in the town, if one didn't count the stationery stores that sold school textbooks and the two handcarts that dealt in old books. I couldn't miss the Teja Bapa *annakshetra*, a free-food kitchen for the needy, and the community kitchen of Dawoodi Bohras, from where about 150 families procured their meals every month at a throwaway price of 1,750 rupees.

Dhoraji was famous for three things, according to the proprietor of Ambika Hotel, where I had my meals: ganthia, *gaffar* and *ganda* – a fried snack, forgivers and lunatics, respectively. Considering Kathiawar's craze for ganthia, I often wonder, wouldn't it have been more appropriate to name it Ganthiawar? The festival of Janmashtami was celebrated with greater gusto than Diwali. People, it seemed, hadn't forgotten the gambling gala of Shravan and swooning fairs, held around the birth of Lord Krishna. There, the Dalits celebrated all Hindu festivals; those responding to a phone call with the greeting 'Namo Buddhaya' celebrated the Buddha Jayanti and Ambedkar Jayanti additionally. But most interestingly, they celebrated Republic Day in front of the bust of Dr Ambedkar. There were temples galore but the ones I developed a huge liking for were Chirag-e-Mamasaheb and Mojila Mamasaheb. Mamasaheb was nothing but the khejri tree under which women prayed for the safety and health of their kids. Khejri trees are disappearing fast and, thus, what remains are these temples of Mamasaheb that dot the whole of Saurashtra. Just like temples, Dhoraji had an abundance of halls, about fifty in all, divided along caste, sub-caste and communal lines. Thankfully, Dalits and Muslims could freely hire any of these spaces to organize their social events and family functions.

In the last days of September 2017, while this was being written and the assembly elections were just round the corner, the political slogan of *vikas gando thayo chhe* [development has gone nuts] had gone viral in Dhoraji too. I had seen with naked eyes how vikas in Dhoraji had gone nuts and how everything was caught in its chokehold. A Dhoraji famous for farming cotton and groundnuts today got potable water for just half an hour a day, five days a week throughout the year. Ironically, the air turned festive in the whole area around the time of water supply. All the talk about round-the-clock electricity supply sounded hollow in the town, which was subjected every Wednesday to a six-hour-long mandatory cut. How can I forget those nights, spent without a wink of sleep, sweating in the humid air, on account of recurrent monsoon outages? And yet, people of Dhoraji, when faced with a pleasantry like 'How are you?', invariably responded with 'In fine fettle, indeed!'

The farewell party for my retirement, organized by my colleagues and friends, was a lot more than a formality. It was an expression of genuine warmth and affection. No wonder I kept receiving messages like 'We miss you!' for days thereafter. A famous *doha*, celebrating the great tradition of Kathiawari hospitality goes,

> 'O lord! Just lose your way someday to Kathiawar
> Be my guest, O Shamala, to have a taste of heaven.'

Neither did I lose my way in Dhoraji nor was I Shamalo, the dark-skinned god. This was just an all-too-human experience, an experience that triggered mixed feelings in me about those years in Dhoraji.

11

Sick Homes: A Journey from Life's Dawn to Dusk

In a fortnight of the proclamation of nationwide lockdown, imposed at a four-hour notice to contain the spread of the coronavirus, a rumour got about that caught by the deadly bug, I had popped off. Throughout the afternoon that day, family and friends, some of whom had not been in touch for many years, rang up to ask if it was true. Ironically enough, it was I who had to tell them that there was no truth in the rumour and that I was alive. Subsequently, the same thing, the farce and fiasco, happened two more times. The first time the rumour flew about, I was completely shaken. (Hearing of your death does that to you.) For this was a face-off with death, qualitatively different from the ones I'd had in the last two years at various hospitals. But by the second and the third time, the game had taken my fancy; it was great fun hearing the wild rumour with a feigned interest and then scotching it, much to the caller's embarrassment. But the suspicion and the concern of those well-wishers about my health was not completely out of place.

Truth be told, my relationship with dispensaries and hospitals is as old as I am. A six-decade-strong bond. It was the rain-soaked evening of July 1959. I was about twenty days old, the fourth child of my mother who was down with puerperal bacterial infection. Suddenly, I started having epileptic fits. Rajpur of those days didn't have a single doctor or a dispensary to swear by. The services of the government health centres were best not spoken of, and my fits were going from bad to worse. Under the shield of a single umbrella, Ba and Ma took me to a private dispensary in Gomtipur, but to not much avail. So, without wasting a moment, they made for V.S. Hospital, one of the oldest and most reputed multispeciality hospitals in Ahmedabad. Admitting me immediately as an in-patient, they began the treatment. About three days passed. On the third night, Ma saw Mother Kalaka in her dream. (Why didn't she show up on the first night?) She commanded Ma to observe *badha*, a vow of abstinence, in her name and take her son home. He would be fine and back on his feet before long, she said. I am sure this was just an excuse. For, in those days of abject poverty, Ba couldn't have afforded to take leave from his workplace, and Ma, with the responsibility of our sprawling, joint family on her shoulders, couldn't have stayed with me in the hospital any longer.

Returning from the hospital, Ma ritually broke a coconut and took a vow not to shave off my first hair until I got well, undertook a pilgrimage to Pavagadh and had Mother's darshan. And the very next day, I was alright, fit as a fiddle, as Ma fondly remembered. In those inexpensive days, a pilgrimage to Pavagadh, as the popular saying went, was a matter of *pavali*, twenty-five paise, but my parents couldn't spare even that much until I turned five. On the one hand, the guilt of not redeeming the vow stung her no end, and my health too, she realized, failed every now and then. So, Ma prayed to Mother Kalaka, apologized for her lethargy and hubris and trimmed my hair at home, sparing just a small tuft of hair at the back. An intelligent way of redeeming a pledge, that. By the time Ma was able to manage a pavali for Pavagadh, I had become, much to her chagrin, a hardcore atheist. In a show of supreme arrogance and impiety, I had told Ma about my vow not to visit Pavagadh or to shave my head in this life as a way of keeping her badha perpetually unredeemed. But she was not the one to give in so easily. Later, accompanied by other members of my family, Ma did go to Pavagadh in partial redemption of her vow. With the result that, even today, I carry on my head my first hair, much of which have now fallen and greyed. Further, I don't believe in the mumbo-jumbo of getting rid of hair to mourn a relative's death. So, I am condemned to live with my *babariya* hair and, thanks to the sin of not redeeming Ma's vow, with the painful memories of a slew of nursing homes I was rushed to and discharged from all my life.

The small, stuffy chawl house where I spent more than half of my life had neither an electricity connection nor a direct line of piped water until I turned fifteen. Neither did we have a bathroom nor a toilet of our own for the first two decades of my life in that godforsaken world of squalor, deprivation and disease. Growing up in a large family on a low income, I had come to develop a meagre body, malnourished and susceptible to diseases. Thus, the illnesses and ailments that had sneaked into my body in childhood eventually struck root. The blasted squatters and trespassers occupy it even today. Hardly did a monsoon pass without giving me the gift of malaria and fever; cold and cough were my constant companions, irrespective of seasons; we stuck together through thick and thin. In summers, it was the turn of boils and conjunctivitis to strike me. Smallpox almost killed me once, and cholera, typhoid, pneumonia and jaundice have enjoyed a free and frequent run of my body. As if all the physical suffering wasn't enough, recurrent phases of insomnia and depression have made my life miserable. And after all these years of fighting and resentment, six goddamn decades, I have finally made my peace with vertigo, eye floaters, tinnitus and blood pressure.

In those days, what we had in the name of a dispensary were a municipal Urban Health Centre in Gomtipur and the 'Insurance Clinic', our shorthand for the general hospital in Rajpur, operating under the Employees' State Insurance Scheme (ESIS). While our entire family got free treatment in the latter, the former looked like a corporate hospital to us just because it charged a small token fee. So, whenever anyone in the family took ill, Ma would take them to the clinic. She would identify the doctors there not by their names or surnames but by their physical features and peculiarities. Thus, one was a fatty, the other a blackie, and so on. But her favourite was the toothy who, she believed, gave medicines that hammered the ailment on the head. Be it morning or evening, the clinic would throb with frenetic activity. Animated by the rounds of patients and their relatives from the working-class neighbourhoods, it looked like a street of busy ants. It served pills and powders in small packets of folded newspaper. But if you had half a mind to receive assorted syrups for cough, cold, and so on, you'd better carry a glass bottle from home, unless you wanted a public dressing-down from the compounder.

When a particular illness didn't respond to the treatment of these local dispensaries, Ma would take us kids to the bigger ones. On such days, I recall, she would get up early and prepare tiffin for Ba. Once, Ramanbhai's foot had gone septic not so much because of the small thorn lodged in the sole as because of his notoriously careless attitude. The wound got so bad … just don't ask. Ma figured out that the emergency was real and immediately decided to approach L.G. Hospital in Ahmedabad, which was at least 16 kilometres from our home. Carrying my ten-year-old brother astride her waist and me clinging to her finger, she plodded down. At the hospital, too, we were made to run from pillar to post to complete formalities for surgical procedure. She, an unlettered woman, went through all of it without losing patience or heart and got back home the same way we had done on our way up. Walking down 16 kilometres on a hot, humid afternoon. When Kamalabehn fell seriously ill after her matriculation examination, Ma had stayed for twenty-one days in the same hospital, looking after her day and night without bothering about food and sleep. As the head of healthcare department of the whole extended family, Ma had seen all women – her daughters, daughters-in-law and sisters-in-law – through their deliveries, providing emotional support, attention and care. Seven years back, when I was admitted to the hospital, none but she had stayed over. Again, when one of my cousins, down with a serious medical condition, was put on the drip feed of forty-two bottles of blood over several days, Ma had stood by her like a rock, stopping her from drifting in that difficult phase of her life.

As a patient or a patient's relative, I have had to visit hospitals, both private and public, in Ahmedabad so very often that over the years, I have come to know those places like the back of my hand. This, too, like much else, was my matrilineal inheritance. Of being a master in matters of hospital, that is. But such mastery unfortunately comes with a bunch of painful memories that refuse to fade long after. Hardly a week had elapsed after I had finished the final examination for Class 8 when we received the news of Ba's accident. As an oilman, Ba had climbed up a mammoth machine and lost his balance while oiling it. As he fell, his body hit the iron guts of the monstrous machine, and thus, he sustained severe injuries in the abdomen area, including the stomach. Ma and I had stayed for about a month in hospital then. It was my first exposure to the hideous reality of the medical world, a close, spine-chilling encounter. Perhaps on that account, my scarred adolescent mind had dreamt of becoming a doctor and intervene in the system. I had received my grades – 100 on 100 in all subjects except drawing – for Class 8 while we were in the hospital. Topping the class in a private school attended mostly by Brahmin–Bania boys – a huge upgrade from doing it in a municipal school with Dalit–Muslim boys – was certainly a cause for celebration, but, unfortunately, I had to bury that joy within the dead, bland walls of the Civil Hospital.

Pretty late in my life, I got exposed to policies around occupational hazards, workers' rights, and so on. I've written about them at times and even fought for them. But I was too young to do anything when Ba was refused the deserved compensation from the mill management at the time. Conversely, I have also been a witness to how workers in those mills deliberately pushed one of their fingers inside the loom and exacted unjust compensation in collusion with the doctor. Sadly enough, they thought nothing of sacrificing a limb if that helped pay up debts or cover religious and social expenses. Today, many of those mills have shut down, and the glory of the Manchester of India is on the wane. And yet, even today, one is quite likely to run into several men in those working-class suburbs who were driven to choose a life with one finger less.

With the passage of time, Rajpur too witnessed a mushrooming of private dispensaries. Of the diverse lot of doctors, all of whom were non-Dalit and, in terms of qualification, less than MBBS, Dr Dalal stood out for his ingenuity; the man laid string cots out on the public road and put patients on drip there. A brilliant logistical and marketing strategy. After a few years, two Dalit doctors started their practice in Rajpur: Dr Bharat Solanki and Dr Bharat Vaghela. During the anti-reservation riots of 1981 and 1985, a wave of caste affinity had swept through Rajpur, and thus, Dalit residents had briefly chosen to patronize only Dalit doctors, 'our guys', in a show of caste solidarity. Around the time these private clinics were making a killing, two of my seniors, Dr Tiven Marwah and Dr Ashwin Gadhvi, became MDs and opened their private hospitals in Gomtipur and Rakhiyal, respectively. After I landed a government job, public health centres and hospitals eventually dropped out of my go-to checklist; my improved financial condition and dwindling standards of public healthcare were equally responsible for it.

In sixty-one years of my life, I have been hospitalized at least sixty-one times, and it's by no means a rough estimate. I have undergone operations for piles twice. In an accident, I had broken my nose, so it was subjected to plastic surgery. And there were seasonal ailments galore. The reason for my chronic stomach ache, a peptic ulcer, was diagnosed late, and for all that while, fits of vomiting kept ruining the quality of my life. It happened innumerable times that I got ready for office in morning, but shoots of excruciating pain delivered me post-haste to a hospital. I have ruthlessly subjected this immunocompromised body to all kinds of dreadful tests: X-ray, sonography, barium, CT scan, MRI, and so on. And yet, it never occurred to me, nor was I ever counselled in that regard, that I should take health insurance to cover these recurring medical expenses. As a result, a big part of my income went down the drain called dispensary.

One may use clever, hyperbolic phraseology to define these buildings, Temples of Health, and so on, but to me, they have always been Sick Homes, if not purveyors of the Sick Building Syndrome (SBS). For, regardless of the mode of my encounter with them, as an inpatient, an outpatient or a patient's relative, these buildings have bestowed on me nothing but pain and suffering. The state of my mind before the administration of anaesthesia and after its impact wore off has always been extremely sad and stressful. Not that I fear death; it's the fear of illness, more like. Time literally freezes for me when I step into a hospital. Life begins to appear so cheap. When I see operated-upon patients being taken home by their relatives from the third or fourth floor of a shopping centre – whose ground floor is lined with jewellery shops – sans elevator, my heart breaks and my faith in the concept and the reality of urban planning dissipates. I have personally seen how doctors, the alleged Angels on Earth, transmute into dacoits when infinite greed and inhuman gall take hold of them. If I have accompanied my relatives in a goods-train-like government hospital, I have also happened to stay in a five-star-hotel-like heart hospital in Ahmedabad when my younger brother developed heart-related complications.

In her dotage, Ma has reclaimed, perhaps with compound interest, all the care she extended to me during my ailments and hospitalizations all those years. For there has not been a year in the first two decades of the twentieth century when Ma wasn't hospitalized at least twice. At ninety, she didn't have any major health issues, and no surgical interventions except for the removal of cataract. Perhaps, she liked nursing homes more than her home. Thus, she insisted on being hospitalized – in a private one, mind you – for even small, seasonal illnesses. And yours truly stayed with her every time, which is one reason why I developed a deep distaste for medicines and health clinics.

On the morning of 18 January 2019, I had set out from home, hale and hearty, for Nadiad, where I was a visiting faculty in a college of journalism. The plan was to conduct classes and then proceed to Vadodara, where I was to attend a literary festival two days later. But, as luck would have it, I felt a sharp, stabbing pain in the chest in the middle of the lecture. I was rushed to a cardiologist. After resting for a while, I returned to Ahmedabad late in the evening and thought it wise to consult Dr Ashwin Gadhvi, our family physician, for a second opinion. The news of the mild heart attack had been conveyed to my family, so a line-up of people, with a stricken look of those who had just witnessed a murder, received me as I climbed the steps of Gadhvi Hospital in Gomtipur, smiling guiltily. The treatment had hardly begun when I doubled up with pain, not in the chest, but in the stomach. Rounds of throwing up took the hell out of me. An urgent sonography test was prescribed. I was shifted to a private hospital in Maninagar. As a patient, it was my first time in the ICU. At the outset, all oral intake was stopped. All movement was prohibited, so the passing of urine and stool was to be done in bed only. I wondered how my journey from a classroom to a deathbed was just a matter of a day. Next day, I was diagnosed with pancreatitis, which was caused apparently by stones in the gall bladder. I was to be in the ICU for the next ten days all by myself, accompanied only by fellow sufferers in conditions direr than mine. A couple of them passed away as I watched, dazed and horrified. My body was attached to a devilish tangle of tubes and wires. My oxygen level was sinking and, once, the blood pressure shot up to dangerous levels. Surely, I was dying, I thought. But on the seventh day, I was given a drop of water, and it gave a new lease of life to my body and mind. Eventually, I was moved out of the ICU and was allowed to go home only after I'd spent two days without any complaint or complications.

Life was getting back into the groove at Gandhinagar, the city I had made my home about two decades back. People around me too were slowly getting occupied with their work and daily routine. Despite having returned from death's door, I had no serious conception of how fatal my ailment could be. Probably because nobody had apprised me about it. In about twenty days, the pain flared up once again. I was immediately admitted to Aashka Hospital in Gandhinagar. Again, the same rigmarole. A quick and proper treatment by two young doctors brought considerable relief. Any further treatment was possible only after the inflammation in the pancreas was reduced, they said. Another ten days in hospital with all dietary privations and debilitating medication. After that, I spent a month solely on a liquid diet as per doctors' advice. The only way to get rid of stones in the gall bladder is to get rid of the gall bladder itself, I was told. I wanted to avoid surgery as far as possible. But then there was no way out of it. As soon as I felt that my body was ready for it, I decided to go under the scalpel.

The operation was successful, and I was back home in three days. The stitches too were removed on the fifth day. The pain persisted, but then I thought this was natural, post-surgical discomfort. Poor me didn't realize then that Yama, the God of Death, was after me. The doctor had carelessly removed my stitches and then fled to the US for a month. The stitches had become infected, which, according to other doctors we consulted, had to be removed though a surgical procedure. A month passed in dilly-dallying and, by that time, the criminal doctor was back from his trip abroad. He performed the surgery, rounds of dressings and so on. Then the biopsy report of the tissues revealed the presence of the tuberculosis bacteria in my body. And thus, the ordeal got compounded – daily dressing plus heavy medication for TB.

As if this bounty of pain was not enough, the initial pain flared up like original sin. Unbearable pain. Again, the same vicious cycle of hospital, stopping of oral intake and diagnosis. Lo and behold! The goddamn gallstone that had my gall bladder ejected, was not in the gall bladder; it had got stuck in a bile duct. Now, for treatment of this new ailment, I was referred to a gastro surgeon, who removed the gallstone through an endoscopy and placed a stent in my stomach. If only they had identified the exact location of the stone before removing my gall bladder! So much for the magic of medical science and the Angels on Earth! All in all, I had to stay for about forty-nine days in hospital in the fateful year of 2019. During that time, Anju, my younger sister, travelled between Mahemdavad and Ahmedabad/Gandhinagar on a daily basis. Ramanbhai and Atit fought on multiple fronts. After I returned home, Kamalabehn took upon her all the burden of nursing and care with her characteristic compassion and silence. If I'm back on my feet today, it's just because of her.

It's been twenty months since my last surgery, and yet I don't feel I am back to my original, healthy self. Covid-19 has added to the woes of my perennially ailing body. At the beginning of the lockdown, when I approached the doctor with a complaint of cough and fever, everybody, including the doctor, looked terrified. Those macabre days between March to October were heavy on someone like me with multiple comorbidities, both physical and emotional. However, that I could write – and get people to write – for the daily digital issue of *Nireekshak* for sixty-five days, coughing and complaining all the while, is not just a surprise, but a consolation, a big one.

Today, my ever-flourishing medicine drawer has slowly and stealthily elbowed out my bedside bookshelf. Which means that the eventide of my life is in the offing.

Translator's Acknowledgements

'I have nothing to say and I am saying it and that is poetry as I need it.'

– John Cage, *Silence: Lectures and Writings*

As a poet, I find it increasingly difficult to make a statement, let alone pen the poetry of acknowledgement; being an autodidact and gadfly imparts a double whammy to that difficulty and makes the exercise seem even facile. On that account, I am afraid I won't be able to mention many people and institutions in this section. However, I owe a debt of gratitude – and I'm not using the phrase lightly – to Chandubhai whose unconditional friendship and love have proved to be an anchor in these alienating times, capable of stripping a sensitive, thinking individual of friends, family, language, institutions, etc.

This work wouldn't have seen the light of day without the coaxing and boxing I received from Ganesh Devy from time to time. Friendship of such a fine human being is a privilege I prize like nothing else in this world. I am indebted to Tridip Suhrud, Rita Kothari and Supriya Chaudhury for their constant encouragement and guidance. I have learnt as much from their scholarship as from their humanity. I can afford to forget all others but not Dalpat Chauhan, Prabodh Parikh, Himanshi Shelat, Gulammohammed Sheikh, K. Satchidanandan, Githa Hariharan, Gautam Vegda and Mangesh Kale, who have shaped my thoughts directly and indirectly. Special thanks to Mantra Mukim, Ratik Asokan and Raaza Jamshed who carried parts of this work in *Almost Island*, *Equator* and *Guernica*.

Finally, and most importantly, without the unremitting love and unconditional support of Mummy and Pappa, I couldn't have come this far in life. I can't thank Chaitali and Tamanna enough, who stood by me in all my (mis)adventures with a steadfastness that can come only out of pure love.

Notes

Introduction

1. Mohan Parmar and Harish Mangalam, *Gujarati Dalit Varta*, Rangadwar Prakashan, Ahmedabad, 1987.
2. B. Kesharshivam, *The Whole Truth and Nothing but the Truth: A Dalit's Life*, translated by Gita Chaudhuri, Stree–Samya Books, 2008.
3. Dhed or dhedh is a conventional pejorative, a casteist

slur, used for a person of the weaver community. The term, prohibited under law, is used here strictly in a descriptive sense.

4. The suffixes like '-do' and '-yo' in Gujarati, when attached to masculine proper names and signify a certain degree of contempt or endearment for the person addressed depending upon the context. In the essay here, Maheria uses 'Gandhido' as a term of affection, as against 'Gandhiyo' that his mother uses to convey her disdain for the man.
5. Chandu Maheria, 'A Home on Probation', 1996. Enclosed with the invitation card dated 7 June for the housewarming ceremony of his new home, 'Nirant'.

Chapter 1: The Mayor's Bungalow

1. In Gujarati, the feminine address 'Ba' designates either mother or grandma in old school parlance. Similarly, 'Ma' refers to mother, even grandma. But the author notes in parenthesis that they called their father 'Ba'. Perhaps, it was a corruption of the term 'Bapa', which is still popularly used, especially

in parts of rural Gujarat, to address father. Local wisdom here says that Bapa is just a 'pa' (a quarter) of Ba (mother) in terms of love and affection for the child. The way gender roles were reversed in the author's family and community through language is utterly fascinating.

2. Chanotara, the plural of chanorato, is a corruption of the local word 'charotari', i.e., a person from the area called Charotar or Charutar. Derived from the Sanskrit root *charu* meaning beautiful, Charutar signifies the verdant beauty of this fertile land between the Sabarmati and the Mahisagar rivers. However, as a slur, it becomes a reflection of the crassness of people from that region.
3. *Dhe* ... is a conventional pejorative, a casteist slur, originally used for a person of Vankar caste but later extended to all Dalit castes in Gujarat to suggest the polluting work of dragging and stripping carcasses, their caste-based occupation. The use of the term is proscribed by law in Gujarat. The term is used here strictly in a descriptive sense.

4. Love Garden is an ingenious improvisation on Law Garden, an urban park in Ahmedabad, Gujarat. Redeveloped in 1997, the park boasts landscaping, lawns, benches, fountains, pond, and so on. Recently, a gigantic street market of handicraft goods and food has cropped up along the walls of the garden.

Chapter 2: The Frigging Fuss over a Rotlo

1. Ranthan Chhath, an important festive occasion falling in the month of Shravan as per Gujarati calendar, is a preparatory day for the worship of Goddess Shitala to be undertaken the following day, Shitala Satam. As on Satam, all forms of cooking are prohibited, Gujarati families cook all food on the Chhath, and have it cold the next day.
2. A traditional Gujarati sweet prepared in winter, using a great variety of dry fruits, spices, medicinal herbs, and so on. A kind of herbal fudge, an elixir if you will, it is believed to boost immunity and nourish the body.

Chapter 3: That Fellow, Gandhido

1. The suffixes like '-do' and '-yo' in Gujarati, when attached to masculine proper names and surnames, signify a certain degree of contempt or endearment for the person addressed depending upon the context. However, depending upon context, such suffixing also turns the address into a term of endearment. In the essay here, Maheria uses 'Gandhido' as a term of affection, as against 'Gandhiyo' that his mother uses to convey her disdain for the man.
2. The Ahmedabad Textile Labour Association, founded in 1920 in Ahmedabad by Mahatma Gandhi and Anasuya Sarabhai to protect the rights of textile mill workers.
3. Founded in 1934 by Mridula Sarabhai with the support of Mahatma Gandhi, the Jyoti Sangh worked for the emancipation and empowerment of women. It liberated women from the restrictions of domestic life and enabled them to work shoulder to shoulder with men in the Quit India Movement in 1942.
4. Gandhi writes about Rentiya Baras in a letter written to Bapubhai, dated 1 October 1926. 'I recognize no

date as my birth anniversary. I know Rentyia Baras. On that day, everyone should spin, and take a vow that he would spin regularly in future, and wear pure khadi if he has not been doing that.' See The Collected Works of Mahatma Gandhi, Volume XXXI, Navjivan Trust, Ahmedabad, 1969, p. 467.

5. The sangh has lost its sheen now and fallen into a decline that started with the closing of textile mills in Gujarat and the onset of the neoliberal economic regime. So steep has been its fall that the celebration of 100 years of its inception in 2017 was attended by less than 500 people.
6. This popular perception, especially among Dalits, is historically incorrect. Dr Ambedkar was happy with the terms he obtained in the pact and expressed his gratitude to Gandhi for his role in the designing and signing of the pact, something which becomes the headline in the *Bombay Chronicle*. For a comprehensive account of what all happened between them around that time, see Ashok Gopal, *A Part Apart: The Life and Thought of B.R. Ambedkar*, Navayana, New Delhi, 2023.

7. Bhanubhai Adhvaryu (1924–1985) was a freedom fighter, Gandhian activist, an educationist, a columnist and a writer. A major intellectual presence on Gujarati sociocultural scene, he wrote about and fought for the rights of Dalits, tribals and the marginalized. He was famous for his column 'Duniya Jaisi Dekhi Humne' [The World as I Saw It] in *Jansatta* daily. Chandu Maheria edited a collection of his fiery essays *Rudra Veenano Zankar* [The Clanging of Rudra Veena].
8. *Census 2001*, Statistics South Africa, https://www.statssa.gov.za/census/census_2001/census_in_brief/CIB2001.pdf, p. 10.
9. M.K. Gandhi had announced a competition in 1929 to design a charkha that was worker-friendly, lightweight and more productive. However, the prize money, a mammoth 1 lakh rupees, remained unclaimed in Gandhi's lifetime until a man called Ekambaranathan from Tamil Nadu invented the Ambar Charkha in 1949, which was introduced to the public in 1954 by the Khadi and Village Industries Commission (KVIC).

Chapter 4: Creed, Conversion and Childhood

1. 'Bhai' and 'behn', literally brother and sister, are conventionally suffixed to proper nouns in urban Gujarat as a mark of respect, even fraternity, for the addressee.
2. The term, literally 'local Christian' or 'Gujarati Christian', designates converts to Christianity from the Scheduled Castes in Gujarat. The state government recognizes them as backward class for the purposes of reservations in education and employment as per the central government's guidelines. To understand the wonderful ways in which this religious group has localized Christianity in Gujarat, see Judy Wakabayashi and Rita Kothari, 'Introduction', in *Decentering Translation Studies: India and Beyond*, John Benjamins, Amsterdam, 2009. It begins with the discussion of the Gujarati translation of the Bible.
3. A popular Gujarati children's story by Shambhu Prasad Bhatt in which the king, suffering from a mysterious ailment, is asked by a *hakim* to hunt for

the shirt of a happy man and wear it for a night to regain health he imagines he has lost. His soldiers scour the length and breadth of the kingdom to hunt for a happy man without success. Everybody in the kingdom was unhappy. Finally, one man in rags proclaims that he is happy. The king asks for his shirt, but the man has nothing to wear except a loincloth, which opens the king's eyes.

4. This reminds me of a powerful scene from Saeed Akhtar Mirza's film *Albert Pinto Ko Gussa Kyoon Aata Hai* (1980). Albert's mother is anxious about his youngest son Dominique, who has entered the crime world and entreats with the church priest to help him return to an honourable living. Her husband, a trade unionist, gets beaten by the goons hired by the mill owner, a tactic to break his morale and coerce him into ending the strike of mill workers he is leading. When he comes home, dishevelled and in a tattered shirt, the priest is present there, perhaps on a 'helping' mission to Dominique. Shaken by his father's appearance, Dominique asks the father pointedly, 'Can you "help" him?'

Chapter 6: A Diwali No Less, That

1. Darbar is not a caste, but an honorific used historically in Gujarat and Rajasthan to designate landed nobility like Charans, Kathis and Rajputs. Chieftains of princely states were addressed as 'Darbar' and the tradition continues even today in large parts of these states.

Chapter 7: Your Chappals, Our Skulls

1. At the time in the caste economy of the village, Dalit households and upper-caste households mutually exchanged services and goods as part of an informal contract; the two parties addressed each other as grahak, i.e., customer. Dalits wove fabrics and footwear for the Savarnas and also worked in the fields of their feudal overlords, who in return provided them food and other supplies from time to time. The exploitative nature of this barter economy cannot be stressed enough.
2. Gandhi, who possessed a rare understanding into the

caste universe and poverty of his countrymen, used to build a chappal *parab*, a roadside hut with piles of footwear, for the use of people participating in anti-colonial agitations and rallies. Anyone could borrow a pair at the start of a march and return it at the end. This move sought to reconfigure the public sphere by marrying it to the idea of Swaraj, or self-rule. I am indebted for this insight to Tridip Suhrud.

Chapter 10: Those Years in Dhoraji

1. Today, a multistorey building, housing state government's offices, stands in place of the school.